RAISING ISAIAH

OVERCOMING THE MISCONCEPTION OF AUTISM

Dr. Marcel Fay Williams

INCREASE PUBLISHING HOUSE

Contents

To my Zai,

I realize that I grew up in many ways while raising you. I have been your protector and have always ensured your world was peaceful. You show me every day that faith in God is all I need.

Foreword

My first duty assignment was in Biloxi, Mississippi, where I shared a home with my best friend Marcel and her daughter, Missy. A few years later, Marcel got married and moved to Arkansas. When she called to tell me she was pregnant, I was overjoyed for her.

I vividly remember the birth of my godson. It happened around the same time I received my military orders to Japan. Knowing I would be away for several years, I made a trip to Arkansas to spend a full week with Marcel, Missy, Isaiah, and Henry. I wanted to cherish every moment with them before my departure.

Isaiah was the most adorable baby. As a Newborn Intensive Care Unit Nurse, I already had a deep love for babies, but Isaiah was special. I could cuddle him, kiss him, and hold him for hours—something I couldn't do with my patients.

As Isaiah grew, Marcel and I often talked on the phone about his development. Despite being a third-time mother and a daycare provider, Marcel had concerns about his progress. I would reassure her, saying, "He'll walk when he's ready." We later laughed when she told me he was walking everywhere, keeping her on her toes. However, as time went on, it became clear that Isaiah was experiencing developmental delays.

Being single and without children, I couldn't fully grasp Marcel's challenges. I could only offer my prayers and a listening ear. Yet, Marcel's determination to understand and help her son never wavered. She was relentless in seeking answers and solutions.

This story is about her journey. It begins with a miracle and ends with one, showcasing the highs and lows and the many obstacles she faced. It highlights a mother's unwavering love and the lengths she would go to for her family. Outsiders might not have seen her daily struggles, but this book reveals the mall. The miracles and challenges interwoven throughout the narrative will leave you laughing, crying, and utterly amazed. You'll find hope and comfort on every page.

The book opens your eyes to the struggles parents and families endure when they have a child who doesn't fit societal norms. It also showcases one mother's journey to defy stereotypes and overcome the limitations set by books, medicine, and well-meaning advisors.

"Raising Isaiah" reveals how a child deemed "abnormal" by society can achieve incredible things. You'll gain a deep appreciation for the special gifts children like Isaiah possess. The limitations we set do not have to define their reality.

If you've ever had a child on the spectrum or suspected they might be, this book is a must-read. If you find yourself at your wit's end, going from provider to provider without finding the help you need, you'll find solace in this story. It reassures you that you're not alone in your experiences.

Marcel's journey showcases a mother who followed her heart and instincts to do what was best for her son. It details the struggles of securing the best education for him and helping him become independent. This book affirms that you and your child are okay and that with determination and faith, all things are possible.

By Gillian Calloway

Preface

THE SKY IS THE LIMIT

Do the challenges of parenting ever overwhelm your dreams for your children? Have you set goals for your family, only to find that the path you're on isn't what you envisioned? Have you looked back and realized your journey is harder than you imagined? Life's challenges affect all of us, but they also make us stronger and better than we ever thought possible. Reflecting on your life, you might discover that the trials you've faced are the gems that guide you toward your unique destiny, bringing you wholeness and completeness. These experiences shape your strength, resilience, and ability to nurture your family in ways you never anticipated, ultimately leading to a more profound sense of fulfillment and purpose.

Often, we pray to get God's attention, hoping He listens to us. However, cultivating a close relationship with Him naturally draws Him closer to us. Never doubt whether you pray enough or in the right way for Him to hear you. He hears you, understands what you are saying, and knows what you need. His love for you is unwavering and unconditional, regardless of the circumstances.

In "Raising Isaiah," join me as I delve into the unfolding narrative of my life and the challenges of raising my son, who navigates life on the autism spectrum. Through candid reflections, I explore the intense emotions and my deep reliance on faith in God. This journey invites you to introspectively open your heart to spirituality and embrace the unique differences that contribute to our collective humanity and enrich our world.

Introduction

If you are picking up this book, it's because something about it intrigues you. Whether you're flipping through its pages at the store or holding it in your hands ready to purchase, there's no guarantee you will finish it. This is not necessarily due to the content but perhaps the commitment it takes to see it through. Sometimes, we don't finish things because we fear the outcome or think we already know it, making the effort seem either above or beneath us. Committing to finish this book means dedicating time and mustering the will power to follow through. This book chronicles a life's journey to raise a child in today's society—a child labeled autistic.

Autism is often misunderstood. Unlike Down syndrome, it is not a disability but a different way of learning. This book captures a mother's unwavering commitment to her son, raising him to be confident, strong, intelligent, and respectful, with a love for God and his parents. It is a testament to faith and discovering the extent to which faith can carry you.

"Raising Isaiah" will teach you to view life from multiple perspectives. You will experience the pains, struggles, and triumphs of raising Isaiah. You might know someone—a child with autism, cancer, multiple sclerosis, or other challenges. Perhaps you have a relative or spouse on the spectrum. Since autism was first diagnosed, much has changed. There's a wealth of information and various techniques available now.

By the end of this book, you will have numerous questions and recall instances where you viewed others' children differently. The past misdiagnoses and misconceptions of autism, often treated with medication and misunderstanding, will be addressed. This book will guide you through a range of emotions, making you reflect on the world an autistic child navigates.

Expect moments of surprise and joy. Whether you are new to the world of raising an autistic or differently-abled child, or familiar with it, this book is for you. It will prepare your mind and heart for the journey ahead, empowering you to be more compassionate. This is a book about champions and commitments—commitments to your child, yourself, and God. I hope you enjoy this book. May it fill your heart with new insights and fresh perspectives.

By Suzanne Burgess

Chapter One

IN THE BEGINNING

My Foundation

Author Marcel Fay Williams

Growing up in the inner city of Philadelphia, I had dreams that seemed larger than life, yet the reality of my environment taught me to be resilient. In a neighborhood where self-defense and quick feet were survival skills during turbulent times of gang wars, there were also moments of warmth and joy that defined my childhood.

I have vivid memories of Friday nights filled with soul food dinners prepared by my mom and her friends, accompanied by the soulful melodies of Roberta Flack, Stevie Wonder, and The Jackson 5 echoing through our home. Music was a constant companion, bringing us together in moments of celebration and laughter. Dancing and singing with my family became a cherished pastime, away to escape the challenges outside our doorsteps.

Weekends were equally special spent with my paternal grandparents, who shared our love for music. I can still recall the ritual of placing a 45 record with that distinctive yellow discs on the record player, losing ourselves in the rhythm and melodies that transported us to another world. Together, we danced into the night, creating memories that remain etched in my heart.

These experiences not only shaped my love for music but also taught me the importance of finding joy amidst adversity and cherishing moments of togetherness with those who matter most. They were the foundation upon which I built my dreams and learned to appreciate the richness of life, despite its challenges.

During my first year of college, I found myself frequently reflecting on how my upbringing profoundly influenced my perspective. Growing up without my biological father present, my grandfather played a pivotal role in my life. He stepped in, taking us kids from my mom on weekends and providing a stable presence that I came to rely on.

More than just a grandfather, he became my father figure, imparting invaluable lessons about our family history and the broader spectrum of black history. For him, it was essential that we understood our identity in a deep and meaningful way, rooted in our cultural heritage and the struggles and triumphs of our ancestors.

These teachings weren't just history lessons; they were moments that shaped my worldview and instilled in me a sense of pride and purpose. They laid the groundwork for my journey through college and beyond, influencing how I approached my studies, engaged with my community, and navigated the complexities of identity and belonging.

Those weekend lessons weren't always what I wanted to do at that age, but looking back, they were incredibly enriching. While my classmates were learning the typical narrative in school, I was learning about Sunni Ali Ber, the first king of the Songhai Empire, when they were celebrating Columbus Day. Instead of George Washington, I was learning about the Buffalo Soldiers and the Underground Railroad during Black History Month.

My grandfather, Reginald Westley Maddox Sr., was a pillar of strength and wisdom in my upbringing. As the vice president of the Philadelphia Chapter of the Universal Negro Improvement Association (UNIA) under Marcus Garvey, he embodied a passionate dedication to advocating for our community. His influence on me and my siblings was profound and enduring.

From the age of seven to fourteen, my grandfather took on the role of our weekly teacher, imparting lessons that went beyond traditional education. He taught us not to harbor resentment towards others but instead to embrace our identity and recognize our greatness as black individuals. In a world where mainstream education often overlooked or misrepresented black history, my grandfather ensured we understood our heritage with pride and clarity.

His teachings resonated deeply with me, especially during my early years of college when I began to appreciate their significance. It was eye-opening for my teachers when I brought his perspectives into my history tests, challenging the conventional narratives with a viewpoint rooted in empowerment and truth.

Above all, my grandfather instilled in us a commitment to excellence and equality, despite the historical injustices that persisted. His lessons continue to shape how I approach my studies and navigate life's challenges, inspiring me to uphold our legacy of resilience and determination.

Two pivotal moments have profoundly shaped the person I am today, enriching my life with a blend of faith and heritage. The first transformative moment occurred when I was twelve years old, witnessing my mother's profound decision to embrace Jesus Christ as her Lord and Savior. This spiritual awakening had a profound impact on our family, grounding us in a newfound sense of faith, love, and community.

My mother's journey towards faith marked a turning point that brought us closer together and provided a solid foundation for navigating life's challenges with courage and hope. Her decision resonated deeply with me, instilling values of compassion, forgiveness, and perseverance that continue to guide my path.

This spiritual awakening was the first of two pivotal moments that shaped my identity and perspective. It laid the groundwork for the second moment, which would further enrich my understanding of heritage and resilience, ultimately shaping my journey through faith and love.

The second transformative event that has shaped me profoundly was delving into and learning from the rich tapestry of my ancestors' heritage. This journey of discovery allowed me to uncover the struggles and triumphs of my people, offering a deeper understanding of my identity and roots.

Exploring my heritage was more than just uncovering facts; it was a journey of empowerment. It connected me to a legacy of resilience, creativity, and strength that spans generations. Learning about the challenges my ancestors faced and the victories they achieved instilled in me a profound sense of pride and purpose.

Understanding where I come from has been pivotal in shaping my worldview and values. It has fueled my determination to honor and preserve our cultural legacy while advocating for justice, equality, and respect for all. This journey continues to inspire me to embrace and celebrate the diversity and richness of my heritage, both in my personal life and in my interactions with the world around me.

Today, I stand firm in my faith and knowledge of my heritage. I love God deeply, and I carry with me the confidence of knowing my own greatness. I AM AMAZING, rooted in both spiritual conviction and cultural pride.

My upbringing has shaped me into a woman who values understanding and compassion,especially for those navigating difficult circumstances. At the age of 14, I embarked on my first summer job at a special need's day camp, despite initial apprehensions about interacting with individuals who were different from me. This experience became a pivotal moment, teaching me profound lessons in empathy and patience.

In addition to my work at the day camp, I also cared for my Aunt Jeanne, who faced the challenges of recovering from an aneurysm and losing her short-term memory. I took on the responsibility of traveling across town to tend to her needs—preparing meals, feeding her, changing diapers, and ensuring her comfort with simple acts like combing her hair. Despite the difficulties she faced, I remained dedicated to keeping her clean and content.

These experiences have deeply influenced my character, fostering within me a profound compassion and a steadfast commitment to supporting and uplifting others, particularly those confronting significant challenges. They have reinforced my belief in the power of empathy and the importance of going the extra mile to provide care and understanding to those in need.

Years after settling in at Little Rock Air Force Base and marrying my second husband, I encountered a family in our church facing a challenge I could relate to deeply. They had a six-year-old son named Marcel, (HOW IRONIC), who, like my aunt, faced the daily struggles of autism. Many caregivers had struggled to understand Marcel's needs, leaving his family in a difficult position. With my background as a licensed daycare provider, I offered to help.

Over the course of two years, caring for Marcel became a transformative experience for both of us. Initially, his anxiety in unfamiliar settings was palpable, but through patience and understanding, we developed a bond built on trust and familiarity. Despite never speaking plainly, Marcel found ways to communicate effectively when given the right attention and care.

Today, Marcel is 31 years old, and our bond remains as strong as ever. Reflecting on our journey together, I realize that caring for Marcel not only enriched his life but also prepared me for the challenges and joys of my own journey. It taught me the importance of patience, empathy, and unconditional acceptance—qualities that continue to shape how

I approach relationships and support those in need. Marcel will always hold a special place in my heart, reminding me of the profound impact we can have on each other's lives through understanding and love.

Jeremiah 29:11 (Amplified Bible) says, "For I know the plans and thoughts that I have for you,' says the Lord, 'plans for peace and well-being and not for disaster, to give you a future and a hope.'"

Chapter Two

MOTHERHOOD

In 1983, I married my high school sweetheart at the age of 20. He joined the military two years earlier, after graduating. Our first child, Marcel Lenae`, was born at Scott AFB, Illinois, in 1984. Shortly after, we received orders to Yokota AB, Japan. Unfortunately, my home life was a nightmare, marked by five years of physical and mental abuse. I eventually had enough and called the police. Unable to tolerate the embarrassment, my husband had me sent back to the U.S. on December 28, 1988, six months earlier than when we were supposed to leave. In the military, this is known as ERD (early return dependent), where a spouse or family member is banned from the overseas military base and sent back stateside without the military member. I left my 2-year-old son, David, in Japan with his father and took my 4-year-old daughter with me.

However, my home life was far from peaceful. I endured five years in a physically abusive marriage. Finally, I couldn't take it any longer and called the police. My husband, unable to handle the embarrassment of law enforcement getting involved, had me sent back to the US on December 28, 1988, six months before our scheduled time of return. This process, known in the military as ERD (early return of dependents), meant that I was banned from the overseas base and sent back stateside without him. I left my 2-year-old son, David, in Japan with his father and took my 4-year-old daughter with me.

In 1989, when my ex-husband returned to the States, we divorced. He was granted custody of our son, while I kept our daughter. I found myself a single mom in Biloxi, MS, working at Biloxi Regional Medical Center working as a Telemetry Technician and found a local church that I joined.

A few months later, I moved to D'Iberville, MS, with my roommate and best friend, Gillian J. Grant (Calloway). We dedicated ourselves to church activities day and night while working exhausting twelve-hour shifts at the hospital. The demanding pace and long hours proved too challenging for my daughter, so I left that job and converted part of our home into a daycare center.

The church I was a member of in Biloxi, MS, had many activities I was a part of. One particular time the missionary department and other members of the church traveled to Jacksonville, Arkansas, to support a new church that was starting up in this new city. I went along on this missionary journey. While we waited for the service to start, a seemingly familiar face walked in. He reminded me of Henry, the drummer from the church in Japan, but that was six years ago, so I wasn't sure. I said to my friend T'Angela Rogers, "He looks like the guy who played the drums at my church back in Japan."

Coincidentally, he ended up sitting in front of me, so I tapped him on the shoulder. He turned around, smiled, and then shouted, "Oh my God!" He knocked over some chairs in his excitement. It was Henry. He was now stationed at Little Rock, Air Force Base. We exchanged numbers and began talking and dating. He proposed to me on Valentine's Day after a church service, and of course, I said yes. Our wedding was planned for June 4, 1994, at 2 pm. We married after eight months of dating, and I was happy. I loved that our home life was peaceful. My new husband was gentle with me, kind, soft-spoken, and a hard worker.

With this being both our second marriages, Henry and I discussed whether we wanted more children. I already had a boy and a girl, so I felt content. Henry, who had a 5-year-old son from his previous marriage, was indifferent about having more children. My desire was to travel with my husband and enjoy life with him and my 10-year-old daughter, Marcel. So, we decided we needed some form of birth control. Right before our wedding, I went to my doctor and was informed that I couldn't be prescribed oral contraceptives due to my heart condition. Consequently, condoms were our only choice.

Three months into our marriage, during my yearly physical examination, the doctor suspected I was pregnant. She sent me to the lab for a pregnancy test, but I assured her we couldn't possibly be pregnant because we used birth control every time. When I found out I was a few weeks pregnant,

I was devastated because this was not the plan. I wanted to enjoy being married and travel the world. Let me share why I did not want any more children and what I experienced with the first two pregnancies.

Being pregnant was a joy for me. I actually loved being pregnant and carrying babies in my tummy. I was only twenty-one years old when I had my first child and twenty-three with the second. Throughout both pregnancies, my marriage was very hard, but caring for my babies, taking my prenatal vitamins, and eating well were top priorities.

Let me tell you how I found out I was pregnant with my first child. I was at Scott Air Force Base in Belleville, Illinois, at the base club with my husband and friends. I ordered a Long Island Iced Tea, and it made me feel so sick that I had to ask the bartender for a glass of milk to relieve my pain. Embarrassing! A few days later, I found out I was expecting.

I had a good pregnancy right up until 38 weeks. I had joined the gospel service at the base chapel and started singing in the choir. My first Sunday to sing a solo was during my 38th week of pregnancy. At the start of the service, I felt warm and nauseous, but it subsided. I was able to sing my solo, "Going Up Yonder." Suddenly, I started feeling bad again. I began fanning myself and asking the lady next to me for help.

She thought I was feeling the Holy Spirit, but I told her no, something was wrong, and I needed help.

The fact that the choir stand was behind the preacher meant all eyes were on me, and the service had to stop to deal with me. They called the ambulance, and the paramedics examined me in the pastor's office. As they were checking me, they expressed that they felt toes. Fortunately, the base hospital was across the street, and they rushed me there. When the OB staff examined me, they discovered my baby had one foot coming out and her other foot was hooked in my ribcage with the umbilical cord wrapped around her neck. "We have a footling breech baby on the way," they said. This had now turned into an emergency C-section. She was trying to walk out and do a split at the same time. I was saying to myself, "What in the world is going on? I can't process this so quickly." The medical staff explained what was happening, what was going to happen, and that it needed to be done NOW!

On October 21, 1984, at 5:15 pm, I had the most beautiful baby girl on the planet. How can a baby be born with her hair already combed? She truly was a tiny thing of perfection. She even stopped the church service to make her appearance, and now Marcel Lenae' Randleman had made her debut. That was truly a lot for me to experience at twenty-one.

Now I'm 23 and living in Tokyo, Japan, on Yokota AB. I was late for my monthly cycle but didn't think anything of it. I went for my check-up, and to my surprise, it turned out I was pregnant! Again, I enjoyed being pregnant, knowing I had life inside me that I must nurture and care for. The doctor gave me a due date of November 17, 1986, and I was excited and happy. Throughout my doctor visits, the doctor informed me I would need another C-section since I had one for the first pregnancy. I did not want that again; the healing process was too painful.

He explained that since the first delivery was an emergency and not due to any issues with my body, I could try for a natural delivery if I returned to the states and delivered at a civilian hospital. That was my choice. I checked my flying time to see when I could leave Japan and go back to Philadelphia, PA, to have my son. I headed back to the US in September so I could deliver in November. My new OB team in Philadelphia measured my stomach and did their examinations. All was going well, and we were on track for the last eight weeks.

My doctor at Chestnut Hill Hospital in Philadelphia put me on high-risk status due to my previous pregnancy problems, especially as we were now past the due date. The last few weeks leading up to my due date, I was seen every week to ensure everything was going well. They were not stressed about anything since my vitals and weight were good, and my baby was doing well. Now we were in the home stretch, but my son had no desire to exit on time.

A week past his due date, they asked how I felt. I was good but tired. Another week went by, and we were now into December. I was heavy, but I didn't want a C-section. I went to my appointment, and he was now breech. His feet were not falling out like my daughter's had; they could just feel he was in the wrong position. The doctor said if he didn't turn, they would have to take him by C-section. He mentioned my son was a big boy, in there eating, growing, and he didn't want to come out. Well, here we go again. I never experienced labor pains since Marcel was two weeks early and an emergency C-section.

I was sleeping, and something woke me up at 11:00 pm. "Oh, that was kind of cute," I thought, so I fell back to sleep, and then it happened again. I finally realized at 1:00 am, "I am in labor." I called my sweet mother-in-law, and she picked me up from my grandparent's house, where I was staying while in the states.

Cutting to the chase, I was in labor for 22 hours of horrible pain and agony. My contractions were so intense that I forgot my name. My water had not broken, so they broke it, and he still did not want to come out. Every five minutes for at least 15 of those hours, I was in such misery. My mother-in-law kept rubbing my back to comfort me. I wanted to scream, "Please don't touch me," but I loved her and couldn't say that to her because she was trying to help me. I told the nurse, "My baby is stuck, and he doesn't know how to come out." I said, "It's dark in there, and he doesn't know the way out." The pain was so intense I thought he was coming out from the wrong exit.

In the last hour, they wanted to give me a C-section. Of course, I said, "Yes, I don't care, just get him out, he is stuck." When they talked about that option, he finally decided to crown, and I felt like I wanted to push for the first time. I remember my mindset; I was delusional and scared as they wheeled me from the labor room into the delivery room. When I saw the delivery room, I locked my hands on the wall to stop the bed from going in there. I was terrified. I thought I was going to die in there. The labor pain was stopping my heart from beating. They took my hand down and hurried me in. I remember the doctors saying, "Don't push, just pant so we can make sure he's ready." I could not believe this was happening to me.

After being moved from one bed to another, I finally reached the moment to push. He emerged with his face towards the ceiling, his big blue eyes locking onto mine. At 9 lbs and 22 inches long, David Maurice Randleman Jr. made his grand entrance into the world. Despite my exhaustion, I greeted him with a heartfelt "Happy birthday" before he was gently taken back by the nurse. Reflecting on the mental, physical, and emotional toll of this birth, I resolved not to have more children. The trauma was overwhelming, and I feared for my life during future deliveries. Despite loving the experience of pregnancy, my past births had been too challenging to face again.

Now I'm onto baby number three, and it's been quite an adjustment for me. I'm 30 years old now, and being pregnant again was a surprise, but I've come to accept it with love. During my second trimester, things got complicated. My doctor wanted me to do some tests to check if everything was okay with the baby. I had to do blood tests, ultrasounds (they call them sonograms too), and even amniocentesis. After all that, I found out that my baby has Down syndrome. It's been a lot to take in, but I'm learning as I go.

Chapter Three

I GOT A MIRACLE

In every cell of our bodies, there's a nucleus where genes store our genetic material. Genes carry the instructions for all our inherited traits and are organized into rod-like structures called chromosomes. Typically, each cell nucleus contains 23 pairs of chromosomes, with half coming from each parent. Down syndrome happens when someone has an extra full or partial copy of chromosome 21. This extra genetic material changes how the body develops and leads to the features associated with Down syndrome. Some common physical traits include low muscle tone, small stature, eyes that slant upwards, and a single crease across the palm. Each person with Down syndrome is unique, so these traits can vary in presence and intensity.

I was devastated when I got the news. I kept it to myself at first because I didn't know how to tell my husband that the test showed our baby had Down syndrome. I felt shattered. The emotions were overwhelming. I had just started to settle into married life again, enjoying being a newlywed with my 10-year-old daughter, and now we were facing this life-changing situation with our unborn child.

After a few days, I managed to find the words to tell my husband. I wasn't sure how he would react—whether he'd be worried, scared, upset, or just processing it all. But when I told him, he held me quietly. His silence spoke volumes, letting me know he was unsure of what to do next.

At my next appointment, the doctor discussed the results of the amniocentesis with me. It confirmed that my baby had extra cells on the 21st chromosome, indicating Down syndrome. He went through all the options, including suggesting termination because of the severity of the condition. I was shocked when he even said, "I wouldn't want to take care of a child like this. "Despite the ultrasound showing some abnormalities (like only having two nasal cavities but no nose structure), I found his suggestion of abortion deplorable. It made me question how I would care for my child, but terminating the pregnancy was never something I considered.

During that time, I was working in the Hematology Oncology Department at Arkansas Children's Hospital in Little Rock, AR. On a break, I called Minister Vickie Johnson from my former church in Biloxi and shared what the doctor had told me about my baby. She immediately activated her faith for me, urging me to call Bishop White for prayer. Despite feeling nervous about contacting such a prominent figure, Minister Vickie assured me that he would pray for me if I called him at home.

Taking a deep breath, I dialed Bishop White's number. When he answered, I poured out my heart, explaining the doctor's diagnosis of Down syndrome and asking for his prayers. Bishop White responded by asking me, "Are you ready"? I said, "yes Sir" He began to pray for God to make my baby boy perfect in the womb, just like Jesus was made perfect in Mary's womb. His words struck me because I hadn't even known the baby's gender yet, but now I knew I was carrying a boy.

As Bishop White continued to pray, I felt the presence of the Lord deeply. Even in my office surrounded by colleagues, I sensed a shift in the atmosphere. My faith surged, and I knew everything would be alright. After thanking Bishop White and hanging up, I called Minister Vickie to share the experience. She rejoiced with me, confident that all would be well.

When I later told Henry about the prayer and its impact on me, he too shared in my happiness. We felt assured that God had intervened with a miracle for our family.

My OB/GYN was troubled by my decision to continue with the pregnancy despite his strong advice against it. Many church members suggested I switch doctors, concerned about his recommendations to terminate. However, I chose to stick with the same doctor, reassuring him and myself that everything would be alright. I received prayers for my baby and maintained strong faith in God throughout. It was clear my doctor's Buddhist beliefs didn't align with mine, but I believed he would eventually witness what God could do.

As the months passed, my check-ups remained routine and uneventful. When I finally had an ultrasound to determine the baby's sex, it was confirmed to be a boy, just as Bishop White had prayed over the phone. That prayer was a profound moment in my life, and I always cherish it, giving all glory to God.

Throughout the pregnancy, I kept up with my prayers, work, church activities, singing, preaching, and family responsibilities. Despite many advising me to slow down, I never grew weary of leading worship or spreading the gospel. As my baby continued to grow strong and healthy, my doctor still had concerns, but I maintained my trust in God and followed all medical advice diligently. I took my prenatal vitamins religiously and ate well, balancing everything amidst my active church and personal life. By the week he was due, I felt my energy wane, especially when singing became difficult due to shortness of breath.

On April 7, 1995, two days past his due date, my son finally made his entrance into the world. As soon as he was born, the doctor carefully examined him, checking every detail from head to toe, searching for any signs of Down syndrome. But to everyone's amazement, my miracle-working God had made him perfectly whole. My doctor was visibly puzzled by the lack of expected signs. With conviction, I declared to him, "God healed him, and that settles it. No Down syndrome!"

Chapter Four

ISAIAH'S DEVELOPMENTAL YEARS

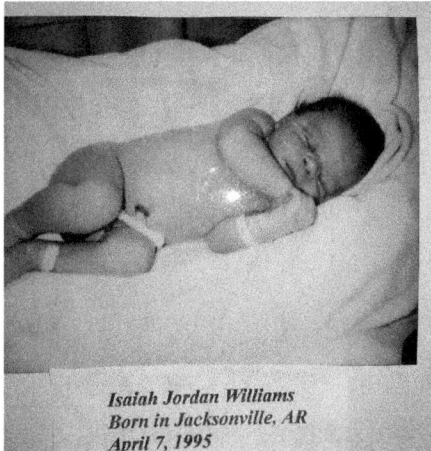

Isaiah Jordan Williams
Born in Jacksonville, AR
April 7, 1995

His name is Isaiah Jordan Williams, my third child, born at 2:52 pm on April 7, 1995, in North Little Rock, AR. He was an incredibly beautiful baby boy, and to me, he was a miraculous gift from God. From the start, he grew at a steady rate, always meeting his size and weight milestones during check-ups. The doctors and nurses adored him for his sweet demeanor and rarely crying. He even amazed everyone by smiling through his immunization shots instead of crying.

However, breastfeeding presented a challenge. His gums were unusually hard, they felt like bricks, making nursing excruciatingly painful for me. It was a struggle that often brought me to tears, and even the doctors were surprised by the strength of his bite. Despite this, Isaiah was a joy and a blessing beyond measure. His peaceful nature and resilience were constant reminders of the miracle he was to our family.

As an experienced mother of three, I was familiar with childhood developmental milestones and recognized early on that Isaiah's development was lagging behind. Around the sixth to eighth month, I noticed he wasn't reaching for objects, lifting his head while on his tummy, or rolling over as expected for his age. His fine motor skills also seemed delayed.

During his well-baby checkup, I expressed my concerns to the nurse, emphasizing that Isaiah wasn't meeting these milestones. However, the response I received was to wait and observe him for further progress. Though I wasn't satisfied with this answer, I understood there was little else they could do at that point. Isaiah was healthy, with a good weight and no signs of distress or discomfort. Looking back, I realize that early intervention might not have changed much, given his overall health and lack of distressing symptoms at that time.

Waiting until Isaiah was two years old to see if there were developmental delays was incredibly tough for me as a mother. Not knowing what was going on with my son and feeling unable to help him weighed heavily on me. I expected professionals in both medical and educational fields to provide answers and guidance on how to support Isaiah, whom I affectionately called "Zai." It was a challenging time filled with uncertainty and frustration. Looking back, I now understand that the support and interventions available were limited, and I realize I was grappling with expectations beyond what was realistically possible.

When Isaiah turned two years old, I eagerly took him to his well-baby check-up, hoping for answers but feeling heavy-hearted. Despite my concerns, my love for him was boundless. Isaiah, with his kind, gentle, sweet, loving, and trusting nature, deserved the world.

At two years old, Isaiah still wasn't talking; instead, he made grunting sounds and pointed to things he wanted. He showed no progress towards potty training, and loud noises made him cover his ears. Leaving the doctor's office that day, I felt just as lost as when I arrived. No one could explain why Isaiah was experiencing delays. Despite his challenges, everyone who met him praised his beautiful spirit and countenance.

Reflecting on Isaiah's journey, I find solace in Genesis 1:26, NIV: ***"Then God said, 'Let us make mankind in our image, in our likeness, so that they may rule over the fish in the sea and the birds in the sky, over the livestock and all the wild animals, and over all the creatures that move along the ground."*** This passage reminds me that Isaiah, like every person, is created in God's image, with inherent dignity and purpose.

When Isaiah started preschool, I hoped that teachers and specialists would have the answers I couldn't find. At three years old, he still wasn't speaking, communicating with grunts and gestures instead. He wasn't potty trained and struggled to interact with anyone outside our family. Despite numerous medical evaluations, doctors and therapists couldn't pinpoint his condition. They observed traits that hinted at autism but not enough for a definitive diagnosis. They likened it to having eight out of ten "marbles." Ten marbles would be considered autism, but since he only had 8 out of 10 we are not sure what his condition really is.

Ultimately, Isaiah was categorized under Pervasive Developmental Disorder Not Otherwise Specified (PDD-NOS). This classification signifies delays in developmental functions like information processing, social skills, and communication. During one evaluation, a psychologist described it as if Isaiah was born without his own thoughts, likening it to having a smooth brain without wrinkles.

Navigating these evaluations and diagnoses was challenging and emotional. I searched for answers while grappling with the complexity of Isaiah's condition, hoping to understand and support him as best as possible.

I tried various creative approaches to teach Isaiah, such as labeling objects around the house. I covered our home with labels so he could learn to read and recognize things. In his bedroom, I even used 3x5 cards to write sight words and taped them to his closet door. Despite my efforts, Isaiah didn't connect the labels and cards with their meanings. For instance, if I drew a circle with two smaller circles inside and a line, you would call it a face, Isaiah saw it as shapes and lines without understanding it to be a face. It was a challenge to find teaching methods that resonated with him and helped him grasp concepts.

Being told by doctors, "We don't know what he is," was incredibly painful and left me feeling lost. If professionals couldn't understand Isaiah's condition, how could I ever hope to help him effectively? His learning style was unique, and processing information posed significant challenges for him.

Processing information was hard for him. I remember feeding him and after he finished eating, I would always say to him, "Are you done?" Then I would take him down from the table. If I got busy after feeding him or took too long to get him from the table, he would start yelling, "Are you done? Are you done?" He processed "Are you done" to mean he wanted to get down from the table. He could have gotten down on his own, but he never did.

Another example of how he processed information is when I was teaching him road safety. Telling him to look up and down the street when crossing were my instructions but it was not the correct information to give him for safety. He would begin to move his head up and down, literally, when he got to the corner, never looking for cars, but obeying instructions. I should have said, "Look both ways to make sure no cars are coming," but even that would have been a lot of information for him to process.

Looking back, I realize how challenging it was to communicate effectively with Isaiah and support his understanding of everyday tasks. His unique way of processing information required patience and creativity in how I approached teaching and guiding him.

Isaiah's way of processing information is unique and requires simplification and clarity in communication. For example, during airport security checks, when asked where he was going, he would respond with "On the airplane," not grasping that they were inquiring about his destination. His mind seems to selectively retain information, liken to a net with tears in it, capturing only fragments of what he hears.

In everyday tasks, such as drying off after a bath, Isaiah demonstrates how he interprets instructions literally. If asked to get his towel and dry off, he might retrieve the towel and wrap it around himself but not understand the next step of actually using it to dry himself. His focus tends to latch onto the first part of instructions, like "get your towel," rather than the entire process.

To help him understand, I've found that using short and direct phrases works best. For instance, saying "Dry yourself off," and "Watch out for the cars," helps him comprehend and follow through with tasks more effectively. Simplifying instructions has been crucial in supporting Isaiah's daily routines and interactions.

Isaiah's social behaviors during his younger years often left me puzzled until I gained more insight later on. In settings where others we reengaged, he sometimes appeared detached, showing little interest in what they were doing. For instance, in his first-grade classroom, he would sit among his classmates but focus on playing with his own truck in a corner, separate from the games they were playing. Despite not actively participating in the games, when they ended, he would enthusiastically suggest, "Let's play again, that was fun!" It was as if he perceived himself as part of the group's activity simply by being nearby.

As Isaiah began to talk, verbal communication posed significant challenges for him. Formulating the right responses to statements or questions was difficult, often requiring him to search for the appropriate words or phrases from his memory. To navigate these difficulties, he taught himself to communicate using movie lines, mimicking the inflection and emotions of the characters he admired. For instance, if he didn't understand something I said, he might respond with, "What are you talking about?" mirroring Woody's line to Buzz Lightyear from the movie "Toy Story."

Isaiah's echolalia, where he echoes phrases by repeating exactly what he hears, remains a unique aspect of his communication style. Even now, if he struggles to find the appropriate words, he may choose to walk away from the conversation without responding. Rather than using straightforward "Yes" or "No" answers, he often opts for more descriptive statements like "I am good" or "I am okay." This preference allows him to express himself in a way that feels comfortable and familiar, reflecting his individual way of navigating social interactions and communication challenges.

Understanding Isaiah's communication style, shaped by echolalia and his unique approach to processing language, has been crucial in supporting his interactions and helping him express himself as he navigates life. Despite being aware of his challenges in reading, writing, and sharp thinking compared to others, Isaiah has never felt limited or excluded from pursuing his interests and aspirations. He has a remarkable ability to draw on creative resources to adapt and compensate for his unique way of understanding the world.

What's truly remarkable is how Isaiah has learned to communicate effectively with me, despite my initial struggles to understand him. His resilience and creativity have allowed him to find innovative ways to express himself and engage with others, showcasing his determination and adaptability in overcoming communication barriers.

There was a time when I realized I could be hindering Isaiah if I didn't change. I did not want him to go outside to play with other kids because I feared he might get lost and I wouldn't be able to find him. I became overly concerned about his well-being, though I thought I was keeping it private, I'm sure others noticed my over-protection too. I had to pray and ask the Lord to help me let him go, to let him experience life like a normal kid and enjoy himself. I did not want to imprison him in the name of love.

The first time I allowed him to go out on his own to play, he didn't come back for two hours and I was frantic. When he finally returned, he was smiling and happy. I asked him where he had been, and he said, "I was with the boy squad." It took me a moment to adjust, but I realized it was okay to let him explore the world. He had a wonderful time playing with the other kids at the playground and in the neighborhood. I saw that my prayers were being answered. Things were working out, and I trusted that God had everything under control.

Chapter Five

I NEED ANSWERS

In November 1997, our family of four received military orders that relocated us to Japan. Amidst this transition, we became participants in the Exceptional Family Member Program (EFMP), a vital initiative that collaborates with both military and civilian entities to offer comprehensive support encompassing community resources, housing, education, medical care, and personnel services tailored for families with special needs. This program proved instrumental in guiding us to bases equipped with appropriate facilities to address Isaiah's educational and medical requirements.

During our time in Japan, we encountered Ms. Patrea, a dedicated case manager within the EFMP who played a pivotal role in our lives. Her compassion and commitment extended beyond professional duties; she became an integral part of our family's support network. Over the span of eight years, Ms. Patrea not only advocated for Isaiah but also embraced our entire family with unparalleled care and empathy. Her exceptional devotion and genuine concern for Isaiah left an indelible mark on our hearts.

Upon our return to the United States and as Isaiah transitioned to new schools, we continually sought to replicate the invaluable support and nurturing presence of "Ms. Patrea" in our lives. Despite our efforts, we never quite found another individual who could match her extraordinary dedication and impact on our family's journey.

Reflecting on the educators and aides who have crossed paths with Isaiah, they consistently admired his demeanor and treated him with a distinct tenderness. Rather than expecting him to keep pace with his peers, many seemed unsure how best to support him, often adopting a nurturing approach that Isaiah perceived as a form of pity. Despite his developmental delay of at least 2 ½ years compared to his classmates, Isaiah saw himself as no different from them in size and height, yearning for acceptance and recognition of his inherent normalcy.

Given Isaiah's unique needs, he repeated first grade twice, a decision based on the absence of clear progress indicators that would justify advancing him prematurely through the educational system. As Isaiah's mother, my priority was to ensure his readiness and provide him with the necessary support at each stage of his academic journey. This approach prioritized his developmental progress over any pressures for accelerated advancement, ensuring that he received the appropriate educational environment and resources to thrive. This decision was crucial in supporting Isaiah's overall development and ensuring that he had a solid foundation for future academic success.

Under the Exceptional Family Member Program (EFMP), Isaiah qualified for a personal aide to assist him during his school day. However, the practical application posed challenges: one aide assigned to five children meant divided attention and frequent shifts between students, akin to a ping pong ball moving from one task to another. This fragmented support structure was inadequate for Isaiah's growth and development in the classroom.

Recognizing the limitations, I advocated passionately for Isaiah to have consistent, dedicated one-on-one assistance tailored to his specific needs. Understanding the logistical constraints and the criticality of personalized support, I eventually assumed the role of Isaiah's classroom aide myself. This decision ensured continuity in his educational support, stepping in whenever the designated aide was unavailable or diverted to assist other students.

In this dual role as parent and aide, I became intimately involved in Isaiah's educational journey, striving to provide him with the individualized attention necessary for his progress and well-being in the school environment.

By the time Isaiah reached his second year of first grade, having had only female teachers who tended to baby him, I recognized the need for a male teacher who could provide a different approach. At Yokota Air Base, where Isaiah attended West Side Elementary School, I found Mr. Jacob Dowdell at East Side Elementary School. I transferred Isaiah there, where he became known as a "Dowdell Dynamo."

Mr. Dowdell didn't see Isaiah's cute face and sweet smile as reasons for special treatment. Instead, he treated Isaiah like any other regular little boy, holding him to the same standards and expectations as his peers. It was a transformative experience for Isaiah, where he was challenged academically and supported in a way that encouraged his growth.

From that point on, I sought male teachers for Isaiah, believing they could provide the structured environment and expectations that he needed to thrive academically and socially. This decision was instrumental in shaping Isaiah's educational journey and ensuring he received the appropriate support and challenge in his schooling.

Isaiah's early affinity for music and rhythm was evident from a very young age, even before he could articulate words clearly. His natural inclination towards playing the drums and keeping beat with songs like Pop Winans' "This Train Is A Clean Train" showcased his innate musical talent. Despite not being formally taught, his ability to synchronize with music was a gift he seemed to have from birth.

As parents, recognizing these natural abilities in children—whether it's painting, singing, playing instruments, or excelling in sports—can be crucial. These talents often indicate where a child can excel and find fulfillment in life as they grow into adulthood. For Isaiah, music became not just a passion but a place where he excelled and felt completely at home.

His early immersion in music, including his fascination with artists like Fred Hammond and Ty Tribbett, demonstrated his deep connection to music and his ability to mimic melodies and rhythms with impressive accuracy. This early passion for music also extended to his ability to dance, a skill that set him apart from his siblings and further highlighted his unique talents.

Understanding and nurturing these innate gifts can be instrumental in shaping a child's identity and future. Isaiah's journey with music exemplifies how embracing and developing these natural talents can lead to a fulfilling career and a deeply meaningful life path.

Reflecting on Isaiah's journey, I've come to realize how crucial it is to nurture all aspects of his development, not just focusing on his challenges with PDD-NOS. During his early years, I was amazed by his musical talents and rhythmic abilities but didn't fully grasp the importance of cultivating them. My primary concern was helping him communicate and integrate into society, which often left me feeling anguished and searching for answers beyond my control.

I see the value in embracing Isaiah's innate gifts alongside addressing his developmental needs. It's a journey of learning and growth for both of us, understanding that nurturing his passions, like music, can contribute significantly to his overall well-being and success in life. My goal remains to support him in becoming the best version of himself, equipped to navigate the challenges and opportunities ahead.

When Isaiah started school and began receiving assignments, it became clear that he struggled to grasp the material and engage with his peers. Despite his cheerful demeanor and willingness to attend, he lacked understanding and failed to connect with others. Ms. Patrea, our case manager, was a compassionate guide during this time, urging me to be patient with Isaiah's slow progress. As he was diagnosed with PDD-NOS, he was placed on an Individual Educational Profile (IEP), marking a significant turning point in our lives.

Managing Isaiah's educational needs alongside navigating the complexities of his diagnosis became overwhelming. I found myself consumed by the challenges of understanding my son and collaborating with professionals. The constant adjustments and new information were difficult for me to process mentally.

Mentally, I felt completely overwhelmed. My husband and I were asked to come to a meeting to discuss Isaiah's Individual Educational Profile (IEP), aimed at aiding his development. Sitting in that boardroom with six teachers and school officials, everything felt surreal. The realization that my son had significant learning challenges hit me like a whirlwind. Tests showed he was below the expected levels in Math, English, Reading, and other subjects. All I could hear was that something was fundamentally wrong with my little boy, and I couldn't hold back my tears throughout the meeting.

Between the tears, I pleaded with them, asking why they couldn't help him. I felt a mix of anger and heartbreak, sitting there surrounded by educators with their degrees, feeling helpless that none of them could unlock my son's mind. In that moment, I realized I was expecting them to perform miracles as if they were divine. The weight of it all was unbearable, and I cried uncontrollably, grappling with the harsh reality of Isaiah's educational challenges.

I struggled to grasp the intricacies of Isaiah's Individual Educational Profile (IEP) after that heartbreaking meeting. Quarterly meetings with the committee became a regular routine, where I returned time and again, hoping desperately for someone to help my son communicate and comprehend.

For thirteen years, I left those meetings in tears, feeling powerless until I had a revelation—I WAS ISAIAH'S TEACHER TOO. I finally figured out I had to be the one to help him with his education along with the teachers, aides, and of course, Almighty God. In my mind, all the progress reports showed no improvement; so, what was the system doing? There was so much paperwork involved, and the system was hard to understand and appreciate. When they explained the plan, they told me, "We have to do something because your child cannot keep up with the others. We will give him an aide, and there will be times when he will be pulled out of this class to go into another classroom, where he will have another aide to give him private time to help him with classwork and to understand what the previous teacher was teaching." This individualized plan they explained was to show how the system works and what they do to change the lives of children. After they told me that, I just knew it was going to fix everything.

Looking back over the 14 years of Isaiah's Individualized Education Plans (IEPs) and the mountains of paperwork I've collected, I can't say I'm impressed. While I know everyone involved tried their best, when I sift through his school reports, I don't see significant overall improvement from the system. Teachers, counselors, and case managers shuffled classes around, but Isaiah consistently remained below average in his learning outcomes. It's not about blaming anyone; it's about reflecting on how challenging it was to decipher those papers and the frustration it caused. Seeing Isaiah's progress reports with his test scores always below average was heart-wrenching, every single time. Even now, thinking about it brings tears to my eyes. I'm immensely grateful to God for being my rock during those times when I felt utterly helpless and sometimes hopeless. I still have all his academic records boxed up in my garage, a testament to his struggles as an underachiever by conventional standards. It was clear they struggled to find the right path for him.

When Isaiah's IEP plan included the suggestion of Ritalin and Concerta, medications typically used for ADHD, the idea was to enhance his focus and attention during school. Ritalin is known for its ability to improve concentration and listening skills, while Concerta, being time-released, was supposed to help him maintain focus throughout the day. Despite following medical advice diligently, these medications didn't seem to affect Isaiah's ability to retain what he learned in class. It was frustrating because Isaiah didn't display hyperactivity, nor did he struggle with staying still in class. It felt like we were trying things out without a clear understanding of how they would help him specifically.

We began with Ritalin, hoping it would help Isaiah focus better in school, but it didn't have any noticeable effect. So, we switched to Concerta as suggested by his doctors. Initially, it seemed like a potential solution, but after a few months, it became clear that the medication was having a negative impact. Isaiah's personality changed, and physically, he started to look different—his eyes drooped, and he had a dazed expression that worried me deeply. It felt like he was being altered into someone else, someone who didn't seem like himself anymore. Seeing him like this scared me, and I realized I couldn't continue with these medications. I decided, NO MORE DRUGS, because I couldn't bear to see him go through such changes. It made me reflect on how much trust we place in others' recommendations, sometimes at the expense of our children's well-being and without fully understanding the consequences.

I've mentioned before how I cried at every IEP meeting for thirteen years straight—it was like clockwork. Those meetings stirred up such immense emotions in me for Isaiah. Crying wasn't something I typically did when I was younger; I believed it clouded my ability to think clearly. In tough times, I always told myself to stop crying and focus on finding solutions. But over the years, my perspective shifted. Learning that God is my heavenly Father I've learned to turn to Him and pour out my heart in prayer, seeking His guidance and understanding in how to best support Isaiah. Now, when the floodgates open, it's not something I control—it's my heart leading the way, pouring out all that love and concern I have for my son.

Chapter Six

TRUST YOURSELF MOM

Zai's journey through youth sports and music

As Isaiah grew older, I supported his passion for sports despite the challenges he faced with understanding the rules. Coaches allowed him to join teams and tried to guide him, but it often didn't work out smoothly, especially from my perspective. While he enjoyed playing basketball with his teammates, he struggled with staying in the right positions, leading to frustrations from others on the team. I found myself reacting strongly from the bleachers, defending him when teammates yelled at him for being in their way. It was embarrassing and not how I wanted to handle things—a pastor yelling at kids. Eventually, I had to find a different approach for Isaiah to participate in sports that would better suit his needs. Each week, Isaiah continued to attend the games, but I realized my emotional reactions were driven by a deep need to protect him. The constant yelling from other kids became increasingly difficult for me to handle. This situation persisted for about two years during our time in Japan. Eventually, I knew I had to find a different way for Isaiah to enjoy sports, one that would be more supportive of his unique needs and abilities, and keep me out of trouble.

Isaiah's early experiences with team sports revealed a challenge in understanding positional play and adhering to structured rules, prompting his transition to a golf camp at the age of eight. Led by dedicated Japanese instructors deeply committed to teaching the fundamentals of golf, they initially underestimated Isaiah's ability to grasp their instructions due to his unique learning style. Despite not conforming to traditional techniques, Isaiah displayed a natural talent for swinging the club accurately, consistently hitting his targets with instinctive precision. This unconventional approach baffled observers, yet it aligned perfectly with golf's individualistic nature, allowing Isaiah to excel based on his personal performance rather than team dynamics. By the camp's end, impressed by his innate abilities, the instructors sought to further nurture his talent, recognizing an intuitive quality in Isaiah's approach to the game. Their appreciation culminated in a heartfelt gesture: one of the instructors gifted Isaiah a set of golf clubs from his personal collection, a gesture Isaiah treasures to this day. Golf emerged as Isaiah's preferred sport, offering him not only a platform for social interaction but also a meditative and relaxing outlet that resonates deeply with his personality.

Ever since Isaiah started taking golf lessons and received praise for his achievements, a newfound sense of confidence gradually entered his world. Previously, he had shown little emotion, whether he performed well or not so well. However, playing alongside others on the golf course began to alter his demeanor as he encountered the competitive nature and rules of the game—concepts that were unfamiliar to him. In his early years, Isaiah had been consistently applauded, experiencing praise as the norm. Despite these new challenges, we have never ceased to encourage him, steadfast in our support regardless of his endeavors.

Throughout Isaiah's early life, he rarely displayed signs of loneliness or longing for others. As a young child, he appeared remarkably self-sufficient, never crying for attention or showing fear. He didn't seem to miss me when I went away, which was convenient for me, because I had pastoral duties that took me across various countries and states. Despite this independence, I often took Isaiah along with me on my travels because he was my son and easy to care for.

Reflecting on those years, I believed Isaiah was content when I left him at home due to his apparent lack of emotional reaction. However, I later realized I had misunderstood his need for connection. Although he didn't express himself in conventional ways and seemed comfortable alone, Isaiah did depend on me in his own quiet manner. Moving back to the United States brought this truth to light, revealing that despite his outward demeanor, he did think about me and missed me when I was away.

When Isaiah was 10 years old, I left him in Okinawa, Japan with his father for two months while I returned to the United

States to search for a home. Throughout that time, he didn't express any feelings about my absence. However, four years later during Bible Study, I was teaching a lesson on how the Lord is a healer and will help you through any hard times we may have. I asked the class if anyone had a testimony of how the Lord brought them through a hard time in their life and if they wanted to share it with the class. Out of nowhere, my now 14-year-old son yelled out, "Yeah, when you left me with him," (pointing to his father), "and you probably gave him papers on me." I was shocked and surprised at his outburst. The class looked just as surprised as I was. Gave him papers? I had no idea what that meant. During the writing of this book, I asked Isaiah about that statement. Twelve years later he told me, that was a statement that came from a sitcom he watched on TV about a couple who went through a divorce and they were sitting in the therapist's office discussing what would happen to the kids. I had no idea he had feelings like that. This was the first time he had ever expressed grief or pain. He never said don't go, nor ever asked me to stay. He never showed signs of loneliness or wanting me to be around. In retrospect, I took care of every need he had for ten years without fail; I should have realized he would miss me being gone for so long.

This moment was profound because it marked Isaiah's first open expression of grief or pain, even though he had never verbally asked me to stay or shown signs of loneliness before. Reflecting on this, I realized that despite diligently meeting all of his needs over the years, my extended absence had a significant impact on him. It underscored his unspoken need for my presence and care, revealing the depth of his emotional connection and dependency on me despite his outward demeanor.

Moving to Arkansas brought about significant adjustments in my life. With my husband stationed in Japan for another four years, I found myself solely responsible for raising Isaiah. Alongside the search for a new home, I delved into researching schools that could cater to Isaiah's specific needs. It was crucial to find an educational environment capable of accommodating his unique differences.

Having spent eight years in Japan, Isaiah had established his educational foundation. I mistakenly assumed that transitioning him back to the United States and enrolling him in school would be straightforward—a matter of presenting his comprehensive records from his previous schooling.

However, upon entering Isaiah's new school in Sherwood, AR, my optimism quickly gave way to the realization of unforeseen challenges. Despite meticulously preparing and providing eight years' worth of detailed school records, the administration informed me that Isaiah would need to undergo further testing to verify the validity of his academic history. For me, this process was not just a bureaucratic hurdle but a poignant reminder of past struggles.

The scheduling of these assessments marked the beginning of an emotional rollercoaster. It was a journey fraught with uncertainties and unexpected twists as we navigated through the complexities of starting afresh in a new educational setting.

I don't think I wanted to believe that Isaiah wasn't grasping the work put in front of him after all these years. I was just making this a problem I could not solve. I convinced myself it was a problem beyond my ability to solve. Whenever I looked into his little face, my emotions overwhelmed me, and I found myself crying all over again as though I was hearing about his low-test scores for the first time. Why couldn't his mind grasp and retain the information the educational system expected?

It wasn't that I didn't understand, I needed to get involved and support him. I just felt unqualified to discern what he needed. I relied on those with degrees and higher education to provide answers that would help him. Little did I realize, we were all doing our best. The significant changes and the quick results I hoped for were years in the making.

The teachers, counselors, advisors, and supportive friends were all doing their part, and I constantly prayed for guidance concerning Isaiah. I longed for the day when I would wake up and find that he had effortlessly acquired all the knowledge expected of him for his age.

There is a wealth of literature available in libraries and on the internet that offers guidance on parenting, particularly for children with unique needs. I distinctly recall hearing about Dr. Benjamin Spock, a prominent American pediatrician whose book "Baby and Childcare" remains one of the best-selling books of all time. Dr. Spock's foundational message to mothers was empowering: "You know more than you think you do."

Dr. Spock's approach to parenting was revolutionary for its time. He was the first pediatrician to incorporate psychoanalysis into his study of children's needs and family dynamics. His philosophy emphasized that each child enters the world with distinct needs, interests, and abilities. Central to his teachings was the idea that effective parenting involves attentively meeting these individual needs at each stage of development.

While I may not claim to have implemented all of Dr. Spock's methods as vigorously as they may sound, I offer this perspective to shed light on the possibilities for nurturing the precious gift of a child. Trust in your innate wisdom and instincts to foster and guide your son or daughter toward becoming the exceptional individual they are destined to be in this world.

Chapter Seven

AUNTIE C

His musical journey

One of the most impactful moments in my son Isaiah's life, a memory that has resonated with him and myself ever since, happened when he was around six years old and just beginning to speak in sentences. It was during our time at Yokota Air Base when I experienced a profound moment of divine guidance for the Lord. While praying, I distinctly heard the Lord speak to me, urging me to teach Isaiah to pray directly to Him, so he would understand that God hears him independently of me. This revelation overwhelmed me, affirming that God was intimately involved in Isaiah's life.

The very next day, I acted on this spiritual prompting. Holding hands, I guided Isaiah to speak to the Lord himself—asking for blessings, understanding in his schoolwork, and protection. This simple practice of personal prayer became a regular part of Isaiah's life. Prayer was already a central aspect of our family routine, and Isaiah embraced this personal connection with God wholeheartedly.

I truly believe God made himself known to Isaiah. His faith in God has never dwindled, ever! He knows God hears him when he prays and will answer his prayers in due time. I prayed for Zai constantly asking God to heal him, as if he were sick. God spoke to me and let me know Isaiah does not have an illness; it is a DIFFERENCE!

Isaiah knows the presence of the Lord is real and that God's love is his portion. He has a pure heart, loves God, and loves all people. Fo r26 years, Isaiah has exemplified the fruit of the Spirit as described in ***Galatians 5:22-23: love, joy, peace, forbearance, kindness, goodness, faithfulness, gentleness, and self-control. He embodies these qualities every day, loving unconditionally as 1 Corinthians 13:13 teaches us. "Three things will last forever faith, hope, and love-and the greatest of these is love.***

Returning to Arkansas, Isaiah's birthplace, I endeavored to create an environment that catered to his needs. Isaiah had a passion for golf, and I was fortunate to discover a charming apartment situated on a golf course in Sherwood, Arkansas. It was a blessing to be back in familiar surroundings among our old church community. The support and camaraderie we received from our church family reassured me that we were not facing our challenges alone.

Isaiah's experience at Light of the World church in Arkansas seems to have been deeply enriching and supportive, especially in the midst of transitions between schools. The community there provided not just comfort and joy but also an opportunity for him to excel in his passion for playing the drums. Being part of a community of young people who shared his faith and musical interests must have been incredibly nurturing for his development.

Psalm 133:1 beautifully captures the essence of unity and fellowship among believers, highlighting the goodness and pleasantness of dwelling together in harmony. This sense of unity and togetherness is crucial in a supportive community like the one Isaiah found at his church.

Hebrews 10:25's encouragement to not forsake meeting together is also apt, emphasizing the importance of communal worship, mutual encouragement, and support among believers.

These verses resonate well with Isaiah's journey, reflecting how faith and community can play pivotal roles in personal growth and resilience.

Our church life was crucial for Isaiah's social development. Spending so much time at church services allowed Zai to develop his social skills. He loved playing the drums and being around people. As he grew older, he started looking at people when he talked, and the things that bothered him as a child no longer did.

I absolutely believe in divine appointments, and moving to Arkansas was one of them, especially for nurturing Isaiah's gift of playing the drums.

Crystal L. McLean-Radcliff and I were stationed togeth-er on Yokota Air Base, Japan. She met Zai when he was 4 years old and became his godmother or, better yet, a godsend. When we moved to Arkansas, it was exciting to have Crystal stationed at Little Rock AFB nearby. She was also involved in our church as the minister of music and quickly noticed Zai's passion for music from a young age—he had a natural sense of rhythm and could hold a note well when singing. Crystal, who is a versatile musician skilled in keyboards, organ, and drums (her favorite), had quite the musical background her-self. At Grambling University, she was one of only two female drummers to make the Drumline.

In December 2006, Zai's dad got him his first real drum set, an electric one thankfully, so my sleep wasn't disturbed too much! Zai would play those drums day and night—it wasn't uncommon for me to wake up at 2 am to the sound of his drumming. This is the foundation of his gift being perfected. From the moment we arrived in Arkansas with "Auntie C," as he affectionately called her, they were inseparable. Crystal shared his love for music and made every effort to practice with him whenever possible. I remember her allowing him to play while she cleaned the church, joining him on the organ or keyboard for impromptu jam sessions. She enjoyed it just as much as he did. I asked her to share her perception of Isaiah, and these are her thoughts:

"I remember the first time I saw this little, tiny, light-skinned, beautiful baby boy. He might have been four years old, really small, cuter than ever... but never said a word. He loved to just touch and point, but man, could he dance. When the Spirit moved, you could not beat him to the front of the church, but then that was no surprise, his parents were right there praising God as well...it's what he knew. He had a fathomless rhythm set when he was dancing. I began to observe his ability to clap on beat (which is no easy feat for adults during a good Holy Ghost shout). Let him hold sticks in his hand, and he never missed the 2. I was the church drummer, so I was exceptionally observant of his ability to hold rhythms, do air drum rolls, and end up back on the 1 and the 2. He was amazing. I knew he might suffer in other areas, but he had to be a percussion phenom.

I really don't even know how our relationship became so powerful. Thankfully, his mother was my pastor and my friend, so I was able to spend an immeasurable amount of time with him.

Side bar: At the time, I was going through a lot in my marriage; my stepson had just been taken away from us. When I thought I'd never want kids, in one minute I became a mom, and then in the next, I became a mom with a huge void... but then came Isaiah. He became my sidekick. For a while, you couldn't hear a word. He would just tap and point. He was so cute, you just went along with it, but not his dad... LOL—I would hear him say, 'Talk boy talk,' 'Tell me what you want.' Well, for a moment, I went with the enabling and loved to feel him tap my leg and point. I was glad to give in. After a while, he progressed into the 'Disney Phase.' You might ask him a question like, 'Isaiah, are you ready to go?' and he would start singing something like 'I'm late, I'm late for a very important date'(Alice in Wonderland). Or maybe he would fall down, and I'd say, 'Hey Zai, are you okay?' and his response would be, 'Ha, ha, ha, I laugh in the face of danger' (The Lion King). I think you get my point. While some might say that was strange, his responses were always keen. It was something to hear.

His father was in the military, and he was gone a lot. My heart had a void that only God could fill, so we kind of had a place for each other that no one else could fix. I became his 'Aunt C,' drum teacher, and he became my God-given Son—My God Son. When I went to church to practice, he came. This connection overflowed into his life at home as well. We were blessed not to live far from each other, so technically, he moved in; he had his own space, still not much of a talker, but I became very reminiscent of the acts of his dad. I made him talk. I made him talk about drums, but that wasn't hard... as time went on, I saw him blossom more and more in his speech... he'd still have a Disney zinger for you every now and then, though. You couldn't stop him from tapping on things, and he never missed a beat. Music was his everything. He listened to it all day long. I think the connection to Disney helped him as well because every good Disney movie has a great Disney soundtrack, right? He knew every song and every beat to every song.

Outside of the music, Isaiah may be in the house, but you'd never know. He loved to be by himself. There came a time when I remember him getting to where he would be able to go to the playground, and he might go up to other kids, but he still wouldn't really talk, and when he did... Here came Walt Disney again. Imagine how kids responded. Some laughed, some walked away. Eventually, he would just move on. He never showed emotion or hurt. Strange, but man, if we could all function like that, it would be great. He wasn't moved by the jokes or teasing, but his mother sure was (smile). She hated that for him, but I tried to help her and him. It wasn't hard with him because he was never affected—he just wanted to play drums.

After I left Japan, I really missed Isaiah. His mom always made sure he came to visit, and when he did, we still rekindled our music connection. A few years later, they moved to Arkansas where I lived, and I was so excited! Let me tell you, a musician's best friend is a drummer—well, a drummer who can 'stay in the pocket.' This was the most important part of drumming; you gotta stay in the pocket. While Isaiah had learned how to do many things on the drums, he had one problem...he loved to do drum rolls. You may think this is not a big deal, but it is. All of this goes back to Isaiah's ability to not only follow directions but to learn how to play with others. Like a basketball team, everybody in a band has his or her job to perform. I can't get in your lane, and you don't get in mine. A drummer who is out of control is like a wild man running around on the court trying to play every position—not cool! In music, I saw that Isaiah had matured in ability, but not in skill. The great thing was, I also learned that he had the ability to become skillful. I teach all my music students according to Psalm 33:3: 'Sing to Him a new song; play skillfully with a shout of joy.' I remind them that the definition of skill is expertise obtained through continual practice. Now, Isaiah loved to practice, but he wasn't practicing the right things. Although he was delayed, he was not dumb and beyond learning anything, especially music. I could see that in his pre-teens, he was becoming a bit 'attitudinal' about this drum thing. He could pull up drummers online and watch them, and he could replicate anything—but none of this helped him stay in the pocket. What is the pocket? I'm glad you asked. It is the groove—steady beat—no extras—just a solid, clean beat. And so, the battle began...we would start playing, two minutes in, came all these rolls—and I would stop him immediately; 'no, no, no, that's too much—stay in the pocket!' I was beginning to see a character of a young man that did not like to be corrected as much. What he was doing wasn't wrong, but it wasn't right for the group. I believe this lesson really helped develop his ability to now be concerned with other people in the room for once. I would tell him, 'Watch me, keep your eyes on me.' He could no longer go freelance; he had to learn how to follow instructions, even in music. I recall our endless nights of practicing, and me correcting him, and his mom chiming in once or twice that I was being too rough; but one thing she knew, I loved Isaiah. I was his biggest fan, and I wanted him to be able to play with all the great people that I knew God was going to bring him before. Without him obtaining the ability to listen and follow, this could not happen. God gave me the patience and the ability to not only gain Isaiah's trust but also his admiration which allowed him to eventually just do what I say. One day it would click, and he would be the best drummer ever because he knew when to get in and out of that pocket. This transitioned into other instruments. Isaiah had an ear that allowed him to replicate sounds on any instrument as well. He has always been blessed like that. One day he said he wanted a guitar, so we bought him one. I started an all-boys band called Ezekiel's Troop. He was the lead guitar player. I think this also helped him with his social skills because he had to communicate with other musicians. He was singing and playing! All the kids at the church played instruments, so Isaiah soon began to become more vocal and outgoing in ways other than music with them. As for music, I would tell him what to play, and he would find it effortlessly. I never really had to push Isaiah to practice—he did it non-stop. In truth, my playing was better because of him. He grew bigger and musically better, but still, occasionally when he'd talk, you might get a younger version of him—but not in music. Musically, he continued to thrive and amaze us all. His goal was to play at the big church General Assembly with the big musicians, and I knew it was going to happen. He was ready...

My relationship with Isaiah was much more than just music. While his mother was from Philly (unfortunately), I turned Isaiah into a Cowboys fan. His mother and I were two totally different people. Teaching him was a village effort, but I knew my part in his life and his part in mine. I took Isaiah everywhere with me when I traveled. As he got older and began to love sports, we would go to the Thanksgiving games at Dallas Stadium every year! I'd fly in my nephew, and the three of us would have a ball. He knew how to exist outside of the drums, and it became more and more apparent. He was really growing up. To some, late. But for us, right on time.

Their bond lasted for four years without interruption. Crystal dedicated herself wholeheartedly to Isaiah, becoming his steadfast mentor and drummer partner. She ensured that he always acknowledged God for his talents and gifts. Before every practice session, she instilled in him the importance of the "3P's" – Prayer, Practice, and Play. These principles became his routine, reinforcing his commitment to honing his skills through consistent prayer, diligent practice, and joyful performance.

Crystal (Crys) truly was a godsend!

Chapter Eight

STAY FOCUSED

Living in the apartment on the golf course was pleasant, but after seven months, it was time for us to move into our own home. I found a charming house across town that captured my heart, and I was told it had an excellent educational program for Isaiah. Before the move, I scoped out the area and noticed it was a diverse community, with racially mixed families and many military personnel. It seemed like the right place for us.

We settled in Cabot, Arkansas, right before the end of the school year to avoid disrupting Isaiah's education mid-year. I genuinely adored our new home and quickly connected with neighbors. However, as Isaiah started at his new school, we faced familiar challenges. Once again, he had to undergo testing to assess his academic level. Unfortunately, his test scores fell below the educational system standards for mainstream classes. Dealing with this process felt like a repetitive and draining task for me.

I know I keep mentioning his testing and low scores, but it's important to remember that Isaiah was categorized as having Pervasive Developmental Disorder-Not Otherwise Specified (PDDNOS), rather than being on the autism spectrum. If he were officially on the spectrum, there might have been more support systems in place for him, but since he wasn't, we had to continually go through the testing process.

I noticed that in his new elementary school, he was one of only two African American boys, whereas his previous school in Sherwood was predominantly Black. While these observations were noteworthy, they didn't really matter in the grand scheme of things. Living in a military environment, you become accustomed to a multicultural, diverse community.

As we both adjusted to our new surroundings, we were enjoying life, and Isaiah was growing in size and confidence. I constantly talked with him and asked him questions. One day, he came out of his bedroom and said, "Mom, I want to be... when I grow up." This was a huge moment because Isaiah, who often struggled with expressing his own thoughts, had come to me with a clear desire. He said, "I want to...!" It was unbelievable and it shifted my world. I could see my flower was blooming. All the love, support, and emotional investment hadn't fallen on infertile soil.

From that point on, he began to enjoy the company of other children and people. I witnessed the change firsthand. My advice to other parents is: NEVER GIVE UP ON YOUR CHILDREN!

Now it was up to me to ensure his dreams come true. I dedicated my life to putting him first and helping him become whatever he wanted. A few months later, we hit a serious roadblock. Because Isaiah was in an Individualized Educational Program (IEP), our home became the bus stop for the neighborhood children. Each morning, six to ten kids would gather in front of our house, waiting for the bus.

On Friday, January 19, 2007, I looked out the window and noticed there were no children waiting for the bus. I wondered where everyone was and saw two boys from across the street getting into their parent's car instead of catching the bus. I thought it was strange but didn't dwell on it. I kept getting Zai ready for school.

When I opened the front door for Isaiah to catch the bus, he went ahead of me. He turned his head and started to read something on the garage door. As he sounded out the words, "Mooove Nig...," I panicked and yelled, "Get back in the house!" Someone had spray-painted "MOVE NIGGA" across my garage door. I grabbed Zai and brought him inside.

Not one neighbor came to warn me about the graffiti. This explained why there were no children waiting for the bus that morning, oddly enough the bus never showed up as well. They all drove their kids to school instead. Protecting my son became more important than ever. I immediately called the police to investigate this hate crime. Being back in the US for only a year and two months, this incident was a harsh reminder of the racism that still existed.

The event made the local news. I called every news channel in the city. Some refused to cover the story, but a few came out to interview me. The Chief of Police and the Mayor visited me. When I asked if this had happened before, they claimed it was unprecedented in our area. However, a black active-duty Army woman living a block away came to my home, terrified, and shared that she had found a noose hanging in her tree and her gas cut off that same morning.

I contacted the NAACP and Oprah Winfrey. The Memphis NAACP said my incident was vandalism with no evidence of the perpetrator, so they couldn't help. The woman with the noose in her tree didn't want to pursue the case and soon moved to another base. Oprah Winfrey didn't respond.

Locally, nothing was done about the incidents, but the FBI started investigating, according to a January 24, 2007 article. The Mayor had the city repaint my garage door the following week. It was humiliating and embarrassing. I just wanted it removed quickly. Sitting with my friend Tammy, I saw a neighbor pass by and mutter, "Oh, that's a shame." But none of my neighbors addressed it directly. For a week, no children came to the bus stop.

Because of the media coverage, people from hours away came to share their condolences. They knocked on my door at all times, bringing cakes, cookies, fruit baskets, letters, and gifts. My neighbors eventually brought cards, food, and gifts to express their sorrow for what happened. Local churches made me an honorary member, and I became a member of three white churches I'd never attended. In Cabot Wal-Mart, people recognized me from the news and apologized for what happened. I never fully understood why strangers apologized for something they didn't do.

After my garage door was repainted, I moved on. My focus remained on Isaiah's education and helping him through his young life. Without my faith in God, I don't know what kind of mom I would have been. My faith drove me to keep pushing forward for him. He grew so much while living in Arkansas, supported by our church and his Auntie C. Isaiah loved everyone, and everyone loved him. By the time he was ten, he believed everyone was either family or a friend, no strangers no enemies. He would greet and hug strangers as easily as he would hug me.

For example, in Japan, we were at the base exchange, and Zai saw a Caucasian man with his family. He ran over and hugged the man like a family member, startling him. This was the first time I saw him initiate affection toward others, and my heart leaped with joy. However, this new awakening of his behavior also made me more vigilant.

Despite his challenges, Isaiah continued to open up and grow. I watched him closely and saw that he enjoyed interacting with others. His church and our travels played a significant role in his development. My advice to other parents is to never give up on their children. Every child is a gift from God, and with faith and perseverance, we can help them reach their full potential.

Chapter Nine

DIAGNOSIS OF AUTISM

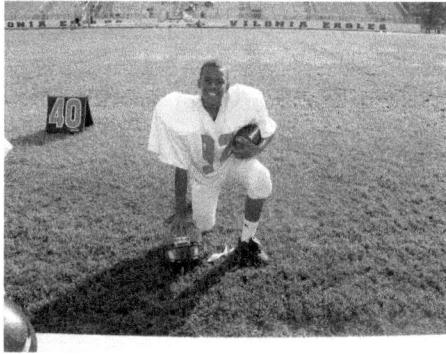

When we lived in Arkansas, we had two small dogs: Tee Tee the Min Pin and Snowball the Chihuahua. I loved them both so much. One Sunday morning before we went to church, I let them out to use the bathroom. Our street was a cul-de-sac, so there was usually no traffic that early on a Sunday morning. Snowball came back, but Tee Tee never returned. Normally, they always came back together. I asked Isaiah to go outside and see where Tee Tee had wandered off to. He carried her into the house, and I saw she had a scrape on her face, but he was holding her in his arms.

I told him to put her down because we had to go to church. When he put her down, she collapsed on the floor, and I realized she was injured. She had been hit by a car, and I was frantic. My heart sank so fast. I could only pray and ask God to please keep my dog until I got home from church. I laid her down on her bed and went to church. I was miserable but trusted God to save my doggy.

As soon as church was over, Zai and I ran out so fast to get home to Tee Tee. When I opened the door, I heard her little bell ring around her neck. I was so happy and got her to the nearest pet hospital. When we got home from the hospital, I asked Zai to show me where he found Tee Tee. He said, "Under the shade tree." My house was up off the street, so I knew there was no tree close to the ground. I asked him to take me to where he picked her up.

We walked down the front steps, and he took me into the middle of the street and said, "Right here." We were standing in the middle of the road. The sun cast a shadow of the tree onto the street. I was shocked and confused by his process. His perspective was interesting; he saw the shadow of the tree as more significant than the street itself, so he picked her up "under the shade tree." A person with a typical perspective would say they picked her up from the street.

By the way, prayer works even for pets. I got her to the emergency room, and the doctor told me to take her home because she was going to die from her injuries. He gave me some pain killers to make her comfortable that night. God blessed me, and she lived 11 more years with no issues except she became a bougie dog. God truly cares about what you care about!

In 2009, we relocated from Arkansas to Louisiana when my husband received military orders back to the US, bringing us to Barksdale Air Force Base. This move marked Isaiah's fifth school transition and introduced him to a new environment in 7th grade. Once again, we navigated the process of enrolling him in a new school and transferring his records. Despite this familiarity, he had to undergo testing to assess his educational needs.

By this point, I had become familiar with the educational system and its procedures. I insisted that Isaiah be placed in regular classes to gauge how well he adapted to the curriculum. I took proactive control over his educational journey because I saw it as my responsibility to advocate for him and guide him as both his teacher and life coach.

During the quarterly IEP meetings, the school would often suggest different strategies and placements for Isaiah based on his test scores. However, I consistently advocated for placing him in a regular 7th-grade class without additional special assistance unless it became clear he needed it. Deep down, I had a sense of what the outcome would be, but I was determined not to accept their recommendations without first giving Isaiah and God a chance to prove otherwise.

When it became evident that Isaiah struggled to comprehend or keep up with the class, I stepped in to support him personally. Whether it meant assisting him myself or filling in when there was a shortage of aides, I made sure he had the help he needed to succeed academically.

As Isaiah became more settled and routine in his life, I felt ready to return to work. I decided to become a substitute teacher for the elementary and middle schools in our area. When I applied, I was offered a position in a special needs class at the elementary school, which I readily accepted.

The class consisted of about ten or more students, each with unique challenges and abilities. It was in this role that I gained first hand experience working with children on the autism spectrum and learned about the diverse range of challenges they face. It was a valuable opportunity for me to deepen my understanding of autism and develop effective strategies for supporting mentally challenged individuals in an educational setting.

After a year of living in Louisiana, the school counselor recommended that Isaiah undergo a comprehensive evaluation to obtain a clear diagnosis of his differences. The school arranged for an independent evaluation conducted by a clinical psychologist in the area. This evaluation was seen as crucial in providing us with a definitive diagnosis and insights into Isaiah's challenges.

As a family, we attended these evaluation sessions because the psychologist also wanted to gather our perspectives on Isaiah. They sought to understand how well we understood his behaviors, weaknesses, strengths, and academic level. Each session lasted approximately three hours, and it was an intensive process that aimed to provide a thorough assessment of Isaiah's needs and abilities.

My husband and I underwent a rigorous evaluation process that included answering a detailed questionnaire with over 60 questions. These questions were designed to assess how we responded to Isaiah's actions in various situations. It felt like we were being tested ourselves, but I understood that this thorough evaluation was necessary to help the clinicians make an informed decision about Isaiah's diagnosis.

During Isaiah's testing sessions, we were not allowed to be in the same room with him. This was to ensure that he could focus solely on the tests without any potential influence or distraction from us, especially me. Over the course of two days of testing, at the age of 16, Isaiah received a diagnosis of being on the Autism Spectrum. This diagnosis came just before our move to Philadelphia.

One thing that became clear to me through this process was that Isaiah was indeed learning, but in his own unique way and with the support of the school system. As we had experienced before, each time we moved to a new state, Isaiah had to undergo testing again. This was because each state and its board of education have their own specific laws and regulations governing education, including how students with special needs are supported and accommodated. Throughout this whole process, I learned how the educational system differs not just from Japan back to the United States, but from state to state, city to city, and even county to county. I also discovered there are different laws and legislation that govern every state's education structure.

Chapter Ten

WHAT IS AUTISM?

Autism is a neurodevelopmental disorder that affects how people communicate and interact with others and the world around them. It's lifelong—you don't grow out of it. Challenges with social interaction and communication are common, but autism can look different from person to person. Autism may also co-occur with ADHD and sensory processing issues. Autism Spectrum Disorder (ASD), or autism, is a complex neurological and developmental disorder that affects how a person acts, communicates, learns, and interacts with others. ASD affects the structure and function of the brain and nervous system. Because it affects a child's development, ASD is called a developmental disorder. ASD can last throughout a person's life. People with this disorder have problems with communication, interactions with other people (social skills), restricted interests, and repetitive behaviors. Different people with autism can have different symptoms. For this reason, autism is known as a spectrum disorder—a group of disorders with a range of similar features.

ASD includes:

Autistic disorder ("classic" autism). Autistic disorder is often what people think of when they think of autism.

Asperger syndrome. Asperger syndrome is sometimes said to be a milder version of classic autism, mostly affecting social behaviors. Unlike people with autism, many people with Asperger syndrome have normal or above-average intelligence and language skills.

Pervasive developmental disorder not otherwise specified (PDD-NOS, or "atypical" autism). PDD-NOS includes some, but not all, of the features of classic autism and/or Asperger syndrome. This category also includes childhood disintegrative disorder and Rett syndrome, two conditions in which a child develops normally for several months or years, then loses skills related to language, movement and coordination, and other cognitive functions.

What Are the Symptoms? The symptoms of one person with autism can be very different from another's. One person with autism may have mild symptoms, while another may have more serious symptoms, but they both have ASD. Despite the range of possible symptoms, there are certain actions and behaviors that are common. In general, the main signs and symptoms of ASD relate to communication; social behaviors; and routines or repetitive behaviors, sometimes called stereotyped behaviors.

Communication: Does not respond to his/her name by 12 months of age, cannot explain what he/she wants Language skills, are slow to develop or speech is delayed, doesn't follow directions, Seems to hear sometimes, but not other times, Doesn't point or wave "bye-bye", Used to say a few words or babble, but now does not.

Social Behavior: Doesn't smile when smiled at, has poor eye contact, seems to prefer to play alone, is very independent for his/her age, and seems to tune people out.

Stereotyped Behavior: Gets "stuck" doing the same things over and over and can't move on to other things, shows deep attachment to toys, objects, or routines, spends a lot of time lining things up or putting things in a certain order, Repeats words or phrases.

Other Behaviors: Has unusual movement patterns, doesn't know how to play with toys, does things "early" compared to other children, walks on his/her toes, throws intense or violent tantrums, is overly active, uncooperative, or resistant, seems overly sensitive to noise.

20 Autism Symptoms You Should Know About:

Autism is a mental health condition that affects an individual's ability to socialize, communicate, and understand abstract concepts. Autism is present from birth and in more than 1% of the population in many countries. Autism is categorized as part of the autism spectrum disorder, which groups together a number of similar conditions including Asperger's syndrome. Autism itself can also vary in severity, with some autistic people struggling with even the most basic communication and others being fully independent and high functioning. For these reasons, it is incorrect to think of autism as an illness to be treated. There is no 'cure' for autism and indeed, many people see it as an important and valuable part of their identity with its own strengths and weaknesses – just like any cluster of personality traits.

There is a lot of confusion and misunderstanding surrounding autism, which can make it difficult to identify, and diagnose. In this list, we will be counting down 20 symptoms of autism, to help better understand the condition and recognize it.

1. Minimal Eye Contact

One of the earliest signs of autism in children is a tendency to avoid eye contact. This is one of the earliest and most fundamental aspects of communication and connecting with others – which are areas that those with autism struggle with. For some with autism, understanding the motivations and thoughts of others is an alien concept. Thus, they may show less interest in the actions or behaviors of others – or might alternatively find maintaining eye contact to be stressful and overwhelming. Some have even described the feeling as 'burning'. In this way, it is now thought that this behavior has less to do with a lack of interest or concern and more to do with a strategy to avoid 'excessive arousal' – perhaps due to imbalances in the excitatory and inhibitory functions of the brain. For parents that notice their young children avoiding eye contact, this is an important symptom to have checked. It might have an alternative point to visual or hearing impairment.

2. Reduced Theory of Mind

As we develop, it is normal to begin acquiring a 'theory of mind'. This means that a child will begin to create internal mental models to predict and understand the behaviors of others based on their interactions. We generally can grasp what another person sees once we have developed past a certain age, simply by observing the direction of their gaze in relation to the world around them (and any items that might obscure their view). In autism, this ability develops later and may never be fully formed. Thus, psychologists will often attempt to diagnose the condition by using tests such as the 'Sally Anne' test. These involve hypothetical scenarios that ask children to predict what characters will do next; based on the information they have available. While many autistic individuals will develop working models of human behavior or coping strategies, they may never gain the intuitive grasp that others do regarding the thoughts and feelings of others.

3. Social Disconnect

For the above reasons, many children and adults with autism will find it harder to connect with others. They might struggle to gain friends, they might significantly prefer time spent alone, or they might find themselves being the victims of bullying. This can result either from a disinterest in forming friendships and fitting in or from difficulty doing so (or a combination of both). At this point, it is important to consider the importance of looking at symptoms in clusters rather than in isolation. A tendency to spend time alone can merely be a sign of an introverted personality type and may have nothing to do with ASD. Likewise, there are also many individual differences among those with autism, with females, they are more likely to form friendships. Those with high-functioning autism will often describe feeling intense and frequent feelings of loneliness.

4. Unusual Speech Patterns

Some people with autism may develop unusual speech patterns. Commonly, this will lead to them sounding both monotone and robotic (with less emotion) or alternatively sounding somewhat 'sing-song'. In some cases, it may appear as though someone with autism is speaking but their tone of voice is not reflective of the content of what they are saying – almost as though they are not fully understanding the way that others might interpret their speech. Autism can also cause a number of other quirks and unusual speech patterns. That said, many autistic individuals will speak normally and maybe highly eloquent. This may be linked with another commonly noticed characteristic of autism: a tendency to pull unusual facial expressions or to grin or grimace. Again, this can be exhibited to varying degrees depending on the individual.

5. Difficulty with Social Norms

High functioning autistics may demonstrate signs of being 'socially awkward'. This can include such things as standing too close, speaking too loudly, or broaching inappropriate subjects. In children, this will often manifest as a lack of understanding regarding usual unspoken social contracts. Autistic children traditions. This can contribute to difficulties making friends, as well as performing in a class where they may find themselves getting into trouble if their condition is not diagnosed.

6. Displaying Lack of Concern

Autistic children may fail to demonstrate concern when someone around them is showing signs of distress. If a friend or caregiver should cry, then they may fail to comfort them or ask what is wrong. Again, this is not necessarily a sign of a true lack of concern – and autistic children do generally form strong attachments with their caregivers. Rather then, this tends to be a failure to interpret and understand the signals that the person is in distress and may require their attention. This may come down to a general inability to recognize specific facial expressions and emotions. Older children with ASD generally perform worse on tests of emotion recognition. Again, this can lead to autistic children struggling to fit in with peers, even if they are eager to make friends. There are some anecdotal reports that autism and ASD may be linked with aggressive or violent behavior. However, this has not been demonstrated by any scientific research and it certainly is not present in all individuals with autism.

7. Anxiety

Those with autism may generally display more signs of anxiety in a range of situations. It is common for autistic children to become anxious when in public, or during changes to their normal routine. Autism also tends to correlate with low 'attachment security'. This is a psychological measure of a child's comfort when being separated from their mother. While most children get upset when they are away from their primary caregivers for extended periods of time, some will find it almost unbearable even to be left in a different room. This trait tends to correlate with a number of developmental disorders, including autism. Other ways in which autistic individuals might exhibit higher-than-average anxiety include reacting badly to sudden loud noises. There appears to be a general link here to 'over-excitation' and so it follows that loud noises should be especially distressing. Parents with ASD also show statistically higher levels of stress.

8. Camouflaging

Camouflaging describes the tendency for some children with autism to attempt to hide their differences. They may do this by studying those around them and learning to try and act in a similar manner and in accordance with what their peers expect of them. This behavior is more common in girls and women with autism than in males, however. While this is understandable, it can also make it harder to diagnose and identify those with autism.

Often, autistic children require understanding and help during school and in their careers – which makes it useful to understand the subtler cues and to address the potential difference in a sensitive and compassionate manner.

9. Poor Communication

Children with autism often struggle with communication from a young age and this may persist into adulthood. In fact, roughly one-third to one-half of individuals with autism will never develop the amount of speech necessary in order to live independently. Some will never acquire any speech at all. Others, however, as mentioned, may fully grasp and master their native language (and perhaps others). During development, infants will often be slower to begin babbling and may babble less frequently once they begin. They are less likely to make requests or respond to questions and likewise may be more inclined to repeat the words and phrases of others (this is called echolalia) or to reverse pronouns. In high-functioning autistic individuals, the grasp of language appears to be somewhat different. Studies show that autistic children will often perform worse at complex language tasks involving figurative speech and inference, however, they might, in fact, have a larger vocabulary in many cases than their 'neurotypical' peers. It may be simplistic to think of this as language impairment, but rather we should consider that it is a different way of seeing and using language.

10. Not Responding to Their Name

Another very early symptom of ASD that parents can look out for is an inability for autistic children to respond to their own names. This may be due to the fact that they don't understand that the name is theirs, or it may be due to a lack of interest in the ensuing communication. Again, this symptom might point to a number of other causes. It can also be a common sign of hearing impairment. In fact, many of the symptoms of hearing difficulties in very young children are similar to those seen in autistic children: an inability to respond to social cues, slow language acquisition, etc. As with autism, it is very important that hearing deficits be identified early on in development, so that children can get the support they need through school. Interestingly, sensory deficits can also be signs of autism in themselves. In fact, sensory 'abnormalities' of some description are found in over 90% of autistic individuals. These difference scan include both 'over-responsivity' and 'under responsivity'. The former is more common though and might result in individuals walking into objects.

11. Obsessive Interests

Itis common for those with autism to display obsessive interests. These might be life-long passions for particular specific subjects such as math, music, trivia, or anything else – or they might be shorter-term infatuations with a particular subject. What might set this apart from a normal childhood behavior is the seemingly random nature of the subjects that the child finds so interesting – and a tendency to talk for long periods on the same topic without considering the other party's interest in that conversation. This is a common be-havior in older individuals with autism, which in turn can serve as another barrier to communication and friendship. In some cases, however, these obsessive interests can also serve the autistic individual well, potentially leading to career paths or helping them to gain impressive amounts of knowledge on that given subject.

12. Savants

One of the most common myths regarding autism is that it necessarily correlates with a higher-than-average ability in math. Famous movies and stories such as "Rain man" have popularized the idea of the 'autistic savant' – cases of remark-able autistic individuals with incredible abilities. The truth is that savants only appear in rare cases. However, it is still a genuine occasional characteristic of the condition – asin cases of 'real-life' "Rain man" such as Daniel Hammett. These individuals demonstrate exceedingly brilliant skills in a range of subjects. Very often these subjects will relate to either math or music: many autistic savants can tell you the day on which you were born from your age and year of birth. Others might be able to play highly complex pieces of music by ear. Memory is also commonly affected, with some autistic savants being able to paint highly detailed portrayals of cities after a single flight in a helicopter. The causes of this condition are not fully understood, but there are many interesting theories. It is possible that savants are merely a natural repercussion of obsessive interests. Alternatively, it may be due to brain plasticity – as language and emotional regions of the brain are underutilized, others see compensatory development. Interestingly, DARPA studies using transcranial direct current stimulation have been able to 'trigger' savant episodes in neurotypical individuals with some success.

13. Self-Harm

Self-injury is a common symptom in those with autism, which tends to affect those with more debilitating versions of the condition. This self-injury can take on many different forms, including eye-poking, hair pulling, head banging, hand biting, skin picking, and more. This can create a significant challenge for caregivers that are thus unable to attend to anything else. This self-harm is generally agreed not to be an attempt at stimulation (as is the case in some instances of self-harm). Rather, it is thought that this is an attempt to help deal with difficult emotions that the individual doesn't fully understand. The self-injury might also be a random tick that happens to have a self-destructive nature.

14. Joint Attention

One of the most crucial aspects of communication is 'joint attention'. In other words, this is the ability to focus on something in particular along with another person. That might mean the ability to follow someone's gaze or their finger when pointing. A common mistake is to look at the finger itself, rather than where it is pointing. This then introduces a mutual point of interest ready for discussion. This missing ability may then go some way to explaining why subsequent developmental stages regarding language can fail to materialize. It can also prevent other basic interactions – such as the ability of a child to point at things they want or to gesture for things they can't reach. Some psychologists believe these actions to be the basis for language.

15. Ticks

A tick is an uncontrolled impulse to move, speak, or make some kind of noise or utterance. These are also commonly present in those with autism and might take the form of twitching, sudden jerking motions, blinking, coughing, or Tourette's syndrome. This behavior can likewise be seen as antisocial and may cause difficulty for the individual in integrating into groups or making friends. However, it is not actually an antisocial activity as such and is rather the result of a more general inability to suppress urges. It might also be linked with other compulsive behaviors.

16. Compulsive Behaviors

Compulsive behaviors in autism can refer to many different things. They may refer to OCD (obsessive compulsive)-like activities: many people with autism will develop rigid routines and 'ritualistic' behavior, which can include checking things, washing often, placing objects in a certain order, etc. In many ways, the character of Sheldon from the series Big Bang Theory actually exhibits a number of common traits associated with autism. Sheldon has very rigid schedules and routines and likes to eat at certain times of the day. Likewise, he will always knock on doors three times, etc. While this is oversimplified and played for laughs, the reality can be quite destructive. Often these routines and compulsive behaviors are very time consuming and thus can end up being debilitating and preventing that person from engaging in normal activities and getting on with their life.

17. Sameness

These compulsive behaviors are closely linked with ritualistic behaviors and a general tendency for 'sameness'. Many autistic people will insist that furniture not be moved. Likewise, they might show a great amount of distress should a friend or relative change their hair cut, or if they should be moved to a different class at school. Again, many of these traits are common in young children and only point to autism when they appear alongside other symptoms that have been listed. Note that there are no single or specific behaviors that are specifically linked with autism. Rather, it is the general tendency to repetitiveness and sameness that is a hallmark of the condition.

18. Difficulty Eating

One of the less commonly known symptoms of autism is difficulty with food. This isn't so much a physical difficulty with eating or refusal to do so but is rather a very specific approach to eating that is tied closely with the sameness and compulsive behavioral traits that we have already observed. Many ASD patients will find that they can only eat specific foods, or once again that they require a large number of ritualistic behaviors in order to eat normally. This can make it difficult for parents to try to encourage a healthy diet and turn dinner-time into something of a chore or a battle for caregivers. Difficulty eating is actually common in autistic individuals, affecting roughly three-quarters of children. There may also be more going on here too though, seeing as many children with ASD also show gastrointestinal problems.

19. Unusual Movement

Another less-often mentioned symptom of autism is motor control issues. It is estimated that roughly 60-80% of people with ASD have motor signs such as poor muscle tone, motor planning problems, and awkward gaits. Thus, you might notice that the individuals walk or stand differently from others, that they make slower and more deliberate movements, or that they seem physically awkward. One commonly observed difference is something called 'toe walking'. These issues are pervasive across all of ASD but are particularly common in autism specifically.

20. Normal Behavior

Okay, this is not a symptom as such, but it is important to remember that autism does not always come with any identifiable symptoms as such. In fact, it is highly common for people with autism to look and behave just like anyone else. And as I alluded to at the start of this book, the differences that do occur are not always things that should be considered 'negative'. We are all different and unique and our brains all work in vastly different ways.

Autism is simply a specific 'type' of difference and one that has some drawbacks and difficulties for those with the condition, but also some unique advantages. This is simply a part of who these people are. There is no 'cure' for autism, just as there is no cure for a quirky sense of humor! In fact, many people with autism or ASD go on to be highly successful. Very recently, an autistic music teacher almost won Britain's Got Talent in the UK with a musical stand-up routine. In order to give autistic children, the best chance of maximizing their natural abilities however, it is crucial that they get the right help and support through school and through life. And that is why being able to identify the symptoms are so crucial.

Chapter Eleven

TESTIMONIAL

A JOURNEY OF STRENGTH AND ADAPTATION

In April 2011, shortly after Isaiah was diagnosed on the Autism Spectrum, my husband retired from 24 years of active-duty military service. A few months later, he took a job in Saudi Arabia, and by the end of that year, I made the decision to move back to my hometown of Philadelphia, PA. Looking back, I believe it was a divine arrangement, as my family needed me more than ever.

Within four months of moving back, my mother suffered her first of three strokes and began experiencing dementia. Despite the weight of caring for my mother and other family members, Isaiah remained my top priority. This move marked the first time since his birth that Isaiah and I had significant time with our biological family and lived in the same city. It provided us with the chance to reconnect with my two brothers, nieces, and nephews, which was a valuable experience for both of us.

Before moving back to Philadelphia, my younger brother Rease had only experienced Isaiah's condition through phone calls and brief visits. Now living in the same state, Rease witnessed Isaiah's life up close and personal. I asked him to share his thoughts:

"I remember speaking to my sister when Isaiah was an infant, and she expressed her surprise and confusion about his developmental skills. Once she identified his condition, she made a conscious decision to raise him with all the love and care

she could provide, despite the odds and limited support. My sister chose to rewrite the book on raising an autistic child when our community had low expectations and was ready to make him another statistic. Isaiah has grown into a kind, thoughtful young man who exceeds our expectations. He is gainfully employed and drives himself to work. It took him four attempts to get his license, but he was persistent. He follows all the rules to the letter, even when I ask him to speed up. It is not Isaiah who needs special attention; he does most things correctly. It is the rest of us who need to learn from him. My life is enriched having Isaiah as a nephew, and I am proud of the young man he has become. No one can take credit for that but my sister, who never gave up on him."

When we moved to Drexel Hill, PA, Isaiah enrolled at Upper Darby High School, which is known for its large student body—over 900 students in his graduating class alone. The sheer size and bustling atmosphere of the school initially overwhelmed Isaiah, but he found tremendous support and growth through their special education program. What stood out most was how they recognized his musical talent; he ended up joining the chorus, which became a real outlet for him. It's amazing how he found his niche in such a dynamic environment.

Dr. Shirley E. Posey, despite being immersed in her doctoral program at Johns Hopkins University, took a keen interest in Isaiah at our church in Philadelphia. Recognizing his potential, she generously offered her time to tutor him during his 12th-grade year. Her dedication and expertise were evident as she shared invaluable techniques to help Isaiah excel academically. Her mentorship made a significant impact on Isaiah's educational journey, demonstrating the power of caring and knowledgeable support in achieving success.

Here are her thoughts...

THE OUTSIDER LOOKING IN....

The brain is the most fascinating organ we have. It's connected and communicates with each other through cells that we call neurons. Those neurons send out these special communications that are electrical and chemical and through that we're able to create this world and understand and perceive this world around us and how we choose to respond to that. Meeting Isaiah, I met his brain and his brain was very special. I think we have to look at brains as if they're individualized people, which they are, and so his brain, I knew communicated differently. But trying to figure out the language in which his brain communicated was one of the master goals that I had in mind because I knew once we figured out how his brain chose to communicate or the language his brain chose to communicate, teaching him certain skills would not be hard. I mean think about it. It's like putting someone in a country where the primary language is Spanish and (yet,they don't speak Spanish). It's going to be pretty difficult to navigate through that country, to make connections with people, to make purchases, I mean even to get a job.

So, it was a key goal of mine to find that language to (flip) on that switch. Through various assessments I determined that he needed a schedule. He needed a schedule to basically help his brain communicate with the outside world and to produce growth.... right! So, a schedule is extremely important because what people realize is that autism doesn't necessarily mean that they lack cognitive ability. Some people with autism are geniuses, they can code. I remember reading an article discussing how they make codes and connections...quite fascinating. It's their social disconnect, right. The schedules that I created for Isaiah helped to basically hold him accountable. Accountability when doing the assessment wasn't because he didn't know arithmetic, again it was a language (Comprehension) barrier. So, going to him and breaking down the mathematical problems visually, turning them into pictures helped significantly and then putting that on a chart...at this time when you get home you are to do mathematics and make it visually stimulating. When he could see that not only did it hold him accountable but it prepared him emotionally for the next step that's going to occur. So, when we look at schedules or what schedules can do or the importance of a schedule, especially with brains that communicate; those such as Isaiah,it supports literacy development. I was able to incorporate words to help him with his development, because that was strengthening him. It also reinforced other things and activities around him and aided in the comprehension of it,and between what was going on in the world around him and then actually what the words meant. Another thing the scheduling helped with was accountability in addition to literacy, and helping to make

a connection with concepts and sequencing. Being able to visually see the schedule and just not hear it, for one it helped and prevented him from becoming frustrated. Not necessarily frustrated because you know Isaiah's brain, he's pretty laid back and relaxed but it helped him to emotionally connect to what was happening and the expectation for

him and it led to responsibility in planning. Things that he could see on the schedule he understood. He understood the expectation, he understood what was going to happen and how it connected and made a connection with his day-to-daylife. It helped him to think about and plan out tasks in appropriate sequencing so that he could have strong executive functioning and execution. So it wasn't like I performed some special magic trick, it was that I turned on a switch andI was able to unlock and figure out the language that he communicated in so that he was able to navigate through the world and all his neurons in his brain that were making his electrical and chemical connections or communications, they were able to determine and navigate in their own world in their own language on their own terms. But then he was able to make sense out of it through the schedule.

Shirley L. Posey

BS Clark Atlanta University

MS Medical Science, Hampton University

Doctoral Student Johns Hopkins University

TEDx Talk presenter

Dana Foundation Brain Awareness Presenter

NashvilleSEL Conference Presenter

Co Founder Neuro Advanced Academics, INC

Chapter Twelve

TIDBITS ABOUT ZAI

- Isaiah's life took a significant turn as he honed his skills as a highly trained drummer. He began receiving invitations from various churches across the country to play at different conferences, which required him to learn how to navigate airports and travel independently. It was a time for him to learn to travel without me, so we embarked on training sessions together. Our travels became practical lessons for him: I entrusted him with tasks such as checking in our bags, tagging them, navigating the automated people mover or train to the security checkpoint, and guiding him in reading his ticket and finding the correct corridors. We always left early to ensure he had ample time to learn without feeling rushed.

- Throughout these experiences, I emphasized the importance of looking for large directional signs and concourse letters. There were moments when we'd stop to eat or deviate from our path, all part of the learning process. Isaiah would walk me to the gate, and we'd sit together before his flights. I felt a mixture of happiness and nervousness, knowing that one day soon, he would travel alone.

- Isaiah's first solo flight at age 20 was from Philadelphia to Little Rock, Arkansas, to play for a meeting at his former church. He navigated the journey flawlessly, never missing a plane or getting lost while traveling across the country. His success was a testament to his growing confidence and independence in managing travel logistics.

- During Christmas, I always wanted Isaiah to have a tree full of gifts since he was my only child living with me. Each year, I would ask him, "What do you want for Christmas?" and he would usually mention one or two items. However, I often ended up buying him ten or more gifts on my own initiative. On Christmas morning, as he unwrapped his presents, he would sometimes say, "I didn't ask for that," and show little interest in playing with new toys or wearing new clothes unless they were specifically requested. Over time, he became adept at articulating his desires, even at eleven years old, while I found myself wanting to give him more than he had asked for. Eventually, I came to understand that he truly was happy with what he asked for. Today, he still prefers only what he asks for—nothing more. This realization not only deepened our connection but also brought about significant savings.

- Isaiah once found himself in an altercation with another child, but upon discovering that the boy was mentally challenged, Isaiah's immediate concern shifted to how he could assist and support him. This incident reflects Isaiah's inherent selflessness and compassion, where he consistently prioritizes others' well-being over his own. Those who know Isaiah can affirm that his presence enriches the world, embodying a spirit of kindness and empathy that leaves a positive impact on everyone he encounters.

- Isaiah's diagnosis of autism occasionally causes me to overlook his physical stature—today, he stands at 5'10" and weighs 260 lbs. He appears like a grown man, yet I always remember the gentle-hearted person within. My former pastor's son, Caleb, offered reassurance that Isaiah's size alone would dissuade anyone from causing trouble. This perspective helped me acknowledge Isaiah as an adult, despite his imposing appearance. Caleb's insight was invaluable in shifting my perception of Isaiah, ensuring I appreciate both his physical presence and his kind nature.

- In Isaiah's 26 years, he has experienced illness only

twice: a single bout of a stomach bug at the age of 12. His medical history is otherwise unremarkable, consisting solely of routine annual checkups that consistently yield normal results. Despite his overall good health, Isaiah does contend with sensory sensitivities, such as discomfort with the buzzing of electric toothbrushes, aversion to excessive physical contact like hugging, and challenges associated with getting haircuts. These sensitivities are notable aspects of his sensory processing, influencing his daily interactions and experiences.

- He is an extremely patient person, always early for work, church, and other commitments. NEVER LATER!

- As the mother of a child on the spectrum, I've encountered a range of reactions from adults. Some express pity, while others have unfairly accused me of laziness or incompetence in caring for him. These hurtful comments, particularly those from a woman after a church service, have been deeply painful. However, I draw strength from my unwavering faith in God and my commitment to my family. Despite the discouragement and judgment, I remain steadfast in my dedication to nurturing Isaiah and ensuring he receives the love and support he deserves.

- Realizing that I couldn't teach Isaiah how to be a man was one of the most challenging moments for me, especially as he turned 18. It was a heartbreaking realization that despite all my efforts, this was something beyond my control. I've often wondered if other women raising sons have felt this same way. Ensuring Isaiah's well-being and his ability to care for himself has always been my utmost priority.

- Isaiah graduated high school in 2014 at age 20. Although legally an adult, I recognize that he may not yet be fully prepared to independently support himself. However, I am committed to never doubting his potential for success in life.

Isaiah finds great strength and inspiration in these scriptures. I pray they bless your life as they have blessed his.
Hebrews 11:1 (AMP):

"Now faith is the assurance (title deed confirmation) of things hoped for (divinely guaranteed), and the evidence of things not seen."

Isaiah's Reflection: "Have faith no matter what the situation looks like. The outcome will always be good. Without God, we wouldn't be here."

Proverbs 18:16 (AMP):

"A man's gift [given in love or courtesy] makes room for him and brings him before great men."

Isaiah's Reflection: This verse means more than just gifts and talents, but Isaiah believes that his dedication to practicing the drums will bring him before great men such as Fred Hammond and John P. Kee. He has met them both and never loses faith in his destiny.

Psalms 150:1-6:

"Praise the Lord! Praise God in His sanctuary; Praise Him in His mighty heavens. Praise Him for His mighty acts; Praise Him according to [the abundance of] His greatness. Praise Him with trumpet sound; Praise Him with harp and lyre. Praise Him with tambourine and dancing; Praise Him with stringed instruments and flute. Praise Him with resounding cymbals; Praise Him with loud cymbals. Let everything that has breath and every breath of life praise the Lord! Praise the Lord! (Hallelujah!)"

Isaiah's Reflection: "We should always give God praise no matter what. I owe God so much for everything He has done for me. I have always loved the feeling of giving God praise, and I do it well on the drums."

Romans 4:17:

"(as it is written [in Scripture], 'I have made you a father of many nations') in the sight of Him in whom he believed, that is, God who gives life to the dead and calls into being that which does not exist."

Isaiah's Reflection: "God can make anything happen for you. Just because you can't see it now doesn't mean it won't happen for you. If God has a plan for your life, He will make it happen for you."

Daniel 1:20 (AMP):

"In every matter of wisdom and understanding about which the king consulted them, he found them ten times better than all the [learned] magicians and enchanters (Magi) in his whole realm."

Isaiah's Reflection: This scripture gives Isaiah hope, knowing that just as these young boys were ten times better than all the other learned men in the region, God would help him become ten times better than he is today. This scripture is what Isaiah spoke on every time he was asked to exhort the people about what God can do for them.

Psalm 139:13-14:

"For You formed my innermost parts; You knit me [together] in my mother's womb. I will give thanks and praise to You, for I am fearfully and wonderfully made; Wonderful are Your works, and my soul knows it very well."

<u>Isaiah's Reflection</u>: Isaiah has always accepted himself and rarely shies away from anything. His core is steeped in his faith in God.

Isaiah's faith and positive outlook on life are deeply rooted in these scriptures. They guide him and give him strength, hope, and a sense of purpose. His unwavering belief in God's plan for his life is evident in his reflections on these verses, and he hopes they inspire others as much as they inspire him.

REMEMBERING:

His favorite song is "Be Encouraged" by William Becton

Be encouraged no matter what's going on,

He'll make it alright,

But you gotta stay strong.

Be encouraged no matter what's going on,

He'll make it all right,

But you gotta stay strong.

I know right now it's impossible to see,

But God is gonna work it out if you just believe.

Remember this one thing while you're going through,

If God delivered Daniel, He'll do the same for you.

Be encouraged no matter what's going on,

He'll make it alright,

But you gotta stay strong.

Be encouraged no matter what's going on,

He'll make it all right,

But you gotta stay strong.

Hold on, trouble don't last always,

These trials are just a test, just a test of your faith.

So stand strong and dry your weeping eyes,

'Cause joy comes in the morning,

And everything is gonna be alright.

Be encouraged no matter what's going on,

He'll make it alright,

But you gotta stay strong.

Be encouraged no matter what's going on,

He'll make it alright,

But you gotta stay strong.

Be encouraged,

Be encouraged,

But you gotta stay strong.

Be encouraged.

A Moment of Innocence and Learning

When Isaiah was around 18 years old, he had a charming habit of coming into my bedroom and hiding under my bed covers. Each time, I would say to him, "Get out of my bed, Isaiah," and he would always wonder how I could see him since he believed he was completely hidden. He had no idea that his body created a huge lump on my bed, making his presence quite obvious.

I tried to explain this to him by getting under the covers myself and showing him how my body made a visible lump, hoping he would understand. Despite my efforts, it did not register with him. It saddened me that, at 18, he could not grasp what I was trying to convey.

This moment reminded me of the unique challenges and learning processes that come with raising a child on the autism spectrum. While Isaiah has achieved so much and grown in many ways, there are still moments that highlight the differences in his perception and understanding. Yet, these moments also serve as gentle reminders of his innocence and the continuous journey of learning and growth we share.

Isaiah's Passion for Cars, Airplanes, and Dinosaurs

Isaiah's fascination with cars and airplanes started early in his life. His dad took him to the Indy Japan 300 while we were living in Japan, which ignited his love for race cars. We often visited Narita Airport in Tokyo where he enjoyed watching planes take off from the observation deck. Isaiah developed a keen ability to identify different aircraft models and was familiar with various airline carriers. Whenever we were at an airport, he eagerly searched the gift shop for new model planes to add to his collection. His room at home was like a miniature runway and speedway, filled with model cars and airplanes.

In addition to his interest in vehicles, Isaiah had a deep passion for dinosaurs. He knew all the different species and would often roam the house pretending to be a dinosaur, complete with dinosaur noises. I joined in his enthusiasm because I shared his love for dinosaurs. His interests weren't limited to machines and prehistoric creatures; he was also a sports enthusiast. He became a fan of basketball and football, developing an impressive knowledge of college and NFL teams, including their colors, mascots, players, and statistics, by the age of twelve. It was remarkable to see how he could seamlessly switch from being quiet to passionately discussing detailed sports information.

Lessons Learned from Isaiah

His Life as a Ministry:

Isaiah's journey has been a profound teacher in my life, illuminating invaluable lessons about faith, love, and the significance of guiding children towards God. His presence has shown me the power of unwavering faith, even in the face of challenges and uncertainties. Through his experiences, I've learned the depth of unconditional love and the necessity of nurturing spiritual growth in children, anchoring them in God's love and guidance. Isaiah has been a testament to resilience and the transformative power of faith, shaping my understanding of parenthood and spirituality in profound ways.

Children are precious to God:

Absolutely, children, regardless of their circumstances or challenges, hold intrinsic value and importance in God's eyes. Jesus himself emphasized the significance of children when he rebuked those who hindered them from coming to him, highlighting their purity of heart and their rightful place in his kingdom (Matthew 19:14). This teaches us to cherish and respect children, recognizing their unique worth and the profound lessons they can impart to us about faith, love, and acceptance.

Training in faith:

Deuteronomy 6:7 (NIV): "Impress them on your children. Talk about them when you sit at home and when you walk along the road, when you lie down and when you get up."

This verse instructs parents to actively teach their children about God's commandments and ways throughout their daily lives, integrating spiritual lessons into everyday routines and interactions.

Proverbs 22:6 (NIV): "Start children off on the way they should go, and even when they are old they will not turn from it."

This proverb underscores the importance of early and consistent spiritual guidance in a child's life. It suggests that raising children in accordance with God's teachings from a young age sets a lasting foundation that endures into adulthood.

Both scriptures emphasize the responsibility of parents and caregivers to impart spiritual wisdom and guidance to children, ensuring they grow up with a deep understanding of

God's principles and a firm commitment to living according to His ways.

Childlike faith:

Matthew 18:3-4 (NIV): "And he said: 'Truly I tell you, unless you change and become like little children, you will never enter the kingdom of heaven. Therefore, whoever takes the lowly position of this child is the greatest in the kingdom of heaven.'"

This passage emphasizes the humility, trust, and innocence that characterize childlike faith, qualities essential for entering and experiencing the kingdom of heaven. Isaiah's faith, marked by his unwavering trust in God despite challenges and uncertainties, exemplifies this childlike faith. His reliance on God serves as a powerful testament to the simplicity and depth of faith that Jesus encourages in all believers.

Personal Relationship with God:

It's beautiful to see how Isaiah has developed his personal relationship with God through prayer. Teaching him to pray and encouraging him to communicate directly with God has clearly been impactful. His initiative to share his prayers with me and seek agreement in prayer shows a deep understanding of the importance of faith and the power of prayer in his life. This connection to God is truly a testament to his spiritual growth and the guidance provided in nurturing his faith journey.

Autism and Relationship with God:

Isaiah's life is indeed a powerful testament to how individuals with autism can deeply connect with God and live out a life of faith, peace, and unconditional love. His journey highlights that autism is not a barrier to experiencing a personal relationship with God or to understanding and embodying spiritual values. Through his example, Isaiah demonstrates the genuine love of God and teaches valuable lessons about faith and perseverance. His ability to forge this connection despite his challenges serves as an inspiration and a reminder of the inclusivity and boundless love of God for all His children.

Autism as a Way of Being:

Isaiah's journey has taught me that autism is merely a different way of perceiving and experiencing the world. He has shown me the importance of relying on God for everything, mirroring his own dependency on me for his needs. Isaiah's ability to remain unaffected by others' judgments and to love unconditionally exemplifies God's love in action. His compassion and selflessness reflect qualities that resonate deeply with the essence of God's love and remind me of the beauty found in embracing differences and trusting in divine providence.

Reflecting on Normalcy:

Isaiah's example challenges conventional notions of "normalcy." His steadfast trust in God, genuine love for others, and indifference to external judgments are virtues that resonate deeply with Christian teachings. In Matthew 6:25-26, Jesus encourages us not to worry about our lives but to trust in God's provision, much like Isaiah does every day. His life exemplifies a profound faith that teaches us to prioritize spiritual values over worldly concerns and to embrace God's guidance with unwavering trust.

Chapter Thirteen

CONCLUSION

I saiah's journey over the past 27 years stands as a testament to faith, love, and resilience. Through his life, he has exemplified the essence of living with unwavering trust in God's love. As I reflect on his growth, I am filled with hope for Isaiah's future—a future where he continues to mature into a strong young man, embodying the fruits of the Spirit and inspiring all who have the privilege to know him.

ACKNOWLEDGEMENT

Thank you, Henry, my darling husband, for your patience and support through the long days and nights of writing this book and taking classes. I always did my best to ensure you were taken care of as much as possible. I love you forever.

Thank you, Gillian Jo-An (Grant) Calloway, for your incredible support in editing my first book. You are forever in my heart and prayers. God sent you to help me, and I know this emphatically. No one could have done what you've done for me.

MEET THE AUTHOR
DR. MARCEL FAY WILLIAMS

I am engaged in various roles as a Pastor, Administrator, Teacher, Author, Educator, and Christian Life Coach, driven by a profound love for humanity. I founded "My Faith Works Ministries," a platform dedicated to imparting strength, encouragement, and healing. This ministry seeks to fortify individuals' faith in God, emphasizing that the measure of faith bestowed upon each believer is ample to conquer any adversity. Romans 12:3 **"For I say, through the grace given unto me, to every man that is among you, not to think of himself more highly than he ought to think; but to think soberly, according as God hath dealt to every man the measure of faith."** underscores the importance of humility and the divine allocation of faith, encouraging mutual support and spiritual edification within the community of believers. By harnessing our unique gifts, we endeavor to meet the diverse needs of our community, promoting spiritual maturation and fostering unity in Christ.

I am the founder of Faith Alliance Consulting, LLC, where I serve as a Certified Life Coach specializing in supporting parents of children on the autism spectrum. Through personalized guidance, I offer comprehensive assistance tailored to the specific needs of each child and family. My services are designed to aid parents in comprehending and navigating the intricate facets of autism. By employing effective coaching strategies, I focus on managing challenging behaviors, improving communication abilities, and cultivating social interactions. My overarching objective is to equip parents with the necessary tools and knowledge to effectively support their children, fostering a nurturing and inclusive environment conducive to their overall growth and development.

I am committed to praying for you through any situation and walking with you through the darkest times. Once I touch your life, you will know me forever. Loving and serving people is my greatest joy. As a dedicated servant in the kingdom of God, I strive to embody Christ's love and compassion in all that I do. My mission is to offer unwavering support, encouragement, and spiritual guidance, helping individuals find hope and strength through their faith journey.

Understanding individuals on the autism spectrum or those traditionally identified as having disabilities necessitates a recognition of inherent differences rather than deficiencies. The diversity of our world is evident in the multitude of human characteristics, encompassing variations in physical appearance, cultural background, and cognitive abilities. Within any societal group, certain individuals may excel due to their intellectual capabilities and swift comprehension, often emerging as leaders who influence and define societal norms.

However, it is crucial to acknowledge the theological perspective that all humans are created in the image of God, as stated in religious doctrines. This divine likeness bestows upon each individual inherent and profound potential. Despite observable differences in physical attributes, cultural backgrounds, or religious beliefs, the principle of intrinsic equality remains paramount. Each person holds equal value as a part of God's creation, and this fundamental equality transcends any superficial distinctions among us.

www.ingramcontent.com/pod-product-compliance
Lightning Source LLC
LaVergne TN
LVHW051240080426
835513LV00016B/1685